The
Mounted
Volunteer

The Mounted Volunteer

A diary of a private of
Missouri Mounted Volunteers on the
Expedition to California, 1846

William H. Richardson

—including—

A Sketch of the Life and Character of
Col. Alexander W. Doniphan
D. C. Allen

LEONAUR

The
Mounted
Volunteer
A diary of a private of
Missouri Mounted Volunteers on the
Expedition to California, 1846
by William H. Richardson
—including—
A Sketch of the Life and Character of
Col. Alexander W. Doniphan
by D. C. Allen

First published under the title
Journal of William H. Richardson

Leonaur is an imprint of Oakpast Ltd

Copyright in this form © 2010 Oakpast Ltd

ISBN: 978-0-85706-166-9 (hardcover)
ISBN: 978-0-85706-165-2 (softcover)

http://www.leonaur.com

Publisher's Notes

Contents

Journal

I left my home on West River, Anne Arundel County, Md., the 11th November, 1845, for a southern tour, and after visiting the principal places of the south and west, inspecting the country, and meeting with adventures familiar to all who travel, I found myself, the following spring, located permanently a few miles from Carrollton, Carroll County, Missouri, boarding in the family of Judge Rea, a clever gentlemanly man. Here I formed numerous acquaintances, among them, an old Capt. Markle, who informed me of his intention to visit California, and depicted in glowing terms the pleasure of travelling in new countries, &c. In the meantime, a company of mounted volunteers was being formed in the neighbourhood, under Capt. Williams, in which many young men whom I knew, had enlisted.

This, together with the enthusiasm which prevailed at a public meeting on the 4th of July, (when the ladies of Carrollton presented the company a beautiful flag, and many speeches were made)—caused me to decide and join the company. I immediately set about preparing—bought my regimentals, canteen, saddlebags, also some books and a writing apparatus for convenience in noting down the occurrences of each day, thinking it probable, should I live to return, it might be a source of amusement to my friends in Maryland.

August 4th, 1846.—This morning we started for Fort Leavenworth. Many of my friends came to take breakfast with me at Squire Dorr's. We met our captain at Carrollton, where a public dinner was given. The company formed and marched to the table in order. In the evening we mounted our fine horses and proceeded out of town. We passed the Prairie, 30 miles wide, and rode as far as the residence of Dr. Arnold. There were fifteen of us in company, separated from the rest, and all in search of quarters.

Having to water our horses, the doctor directed us where to go.

The way was plainly pointed out, but to our astonishment, we all got lost in the timber. We rode till very late, and might have been put to great inconvenience, had we not met with a servant who set us right. We returned to the doctor's to muse on our mishap, and to enjoy more hospitality. An ominous beginning for a soldier's life.

5th.—Started this morning in company with the doctor and his lady, who went with us eight miles to Lexington, and thence to Richmond, where we arrived at 4 o'clock. A few miles further on we encamped. I rode all this day without my dinner. Having had opportunity to become better acquainted with my captain and other officers, I find them very clever and kind.

6th.—I discovered this morning that my horse was lame from tightness of his shoes. Went to town to a blacksmith who re-shod him. The company could not wait for me, and I travelled alone through a beautiful forest of sugar trees. Passed Elke Horn, and rode until within six miles of Liberty. Here I found our baggage team had given out. Our captain had gone ahead with the company, and left the second lieutenant, Mr. Smith, in charge. I discovered Lieut. Smith to be a man of very tender feelings. Several of our company were taken with chills tonight, which is rather discouraging.

7th.—At daylight this morning our train was under way, arrived in town for breakfast, after which our captain marched us all over the city. It is a beautiful inland place of 1000 inhabitants. Fifteen miles further on we met our first lieutenant, just from the fort. He told us to hurry on and get mustered into service before the other companies should crowd in. We hurried accordingly and reached Platt City at sunset. I was fatigued and hungry, and went into the hotel to get my supper; when I came out, I found our third lieutenant had come up with the rest of the men, and were ready to start for the ferry.

I went on with them. We arrived at the ferry, opposite Fort Leavenworth, about 12 o'clock at night. I went in search of something for my horse. There was a widow lady living near, to whom I applied, and she very pleasantly told me "to go to the crib and help myself." I went, fed my horse, and spent the rest of the night on the unhusked ears in the crib, where I slept soundly.

8th.—Rose early and went in search of my captain. Found him, with many others, between some fallen trees, wrapped up in their blankets, fast asleep on the sand. We soon prepared for crossing the river, which I felt to be the bidding *adieu* to friends and home, and almost civilization itself. I was the only one who had taken refreshment. It was fortunate for me that I had made a second visit to the widow and obtained a good breakfast. We were soon all safely over the ferry, 85 in number, men of all grades and dispositions, some very facetious, and others reserved and thoughtful. We were all huddled together, and ordered to form in double file, to proceed two miles from the fort to erect our tents.

We had to wait some time for the wagons which contained our provisions, consisting of mess pork, sugar, coffee, &c. The head of each mess—six in number, had to apply to the sergeant for the necessary supplies. Having been appointed to the charge of my mess, I went up, took my share, and helped the men to theirs. The first meal I tasted in the Indian territory was supper, and such a supper! It was composed of hard water crackers and mess pork, which would cut five inches through the ribs. I boiled my pork for nearly two hours, and found it still so tough that it was harder labour than I had been at all day to eat it. Necessity is the mother of invention, and I fell upon an expedient by which to dispatch it; I took it out, stewed and fried it. But it was yet spongy and stuck in my teeth.

I made out, however, with the assistance of a keen appetite; and being very tired, I laid myself down on my blanket in the tent. I had not lain many minutes when our orderly came by, calling upon the men to form a line. We had much rather slept, but to obey was our duty, and we were soon in the line. We were then drilled by a young officer from the fort. After drill, the officers commenced counting us off from right to left, and every fourth man had to stand guard.

I was taken as one of the fourth men and placed with eleven others at No. 1, where I had to walk my post two hours. It was quite long enough for a beginning, and I resigned the post with pleasure, when the time expired. At 12 o'clock the relief guard put a man in my place, and I went rejoicing to my rest.

Sunday, 9th.—This morning I had to get breakfast for the first time in my life; I was perfectly green at the business, but it had to be done. I filled the kettle with water, browned my coffee, fried the pork, &c. I went on very well until by an unlucky mishap I upset the kettle, and put out the fire. Nothing daunted by the misfortune, I entered upon another trial and was more successful. We paraded immediately after breakfast, and prepared to go to the Fort, where we had the honour of being mustered into service by our colonel. He called our names, and as each passed before him, he was asked his age, and as many other questions as would afford a pretty good description of his person and history of his life. The *Articles of War* were then read, and we formed a line and returned to camp. The roll was called soon after, and all that were not present, had to keep guard. So much for playing truant on an occasion of so much importance. I was fortunate enough to be present, and escaped the infliction.

12th.—The past two or three days were employed in strict attention to the duties of a soldier, such as cooking, drilling, &c. Today, Col. Price assembled the whole regiment at the fort, to have an appraisement of horses, saddles, &c. In the afternoon I rode back to the encampment on a large bag of beef in the hot sun. A severe headache was my travelling companion.

14th.—Yesterday and today we had a terrible job, breaking mules to the wagons. It is difficult to muster these stubborn animals into service. I, with a fellow soldier, was detained from the Fort till a late hour. We were employed in the novel pursuit of pulling two of the mules by main force through the hazel bushes two miles. Only think of it! Two of Uncle Sam's worthies pulling a jackass apiece two miles through the bushes While at the fort I called on the minister, who was very kind and affectionate in his conversation and manners. (He presented me a Testament, Prayer Book, and a bundle of Tracts—at night we threw copies into each tent, and then sung hymns until it was time to retire.

15th.—This was our washing day. I went with the rest of the b'hoys to the branch, where we kindled three large fires, and put up our camp kettles to boil the clothes. I never boiled any before, and I felt pretty much as I did when I began to cook breakfast. I went to work awkwardly enough, as my scalded hands bore witness. But a man can even wash his clothes when he is obliged to do it, the opinions of the ladies to the contrary notwithstanding. In the evening we ceased our labours as washers of clothes, and went into the branch and washed ourselves. After bathing we returned to camp quite refreshed.

Sunday, 16th.—This morning I thought I would hear the Missionary preach—and with several others, started for the purpose. Just before we got to the village, an Indian informed us there would be no preaching that day. We were greatly disappointed, and turned to wander about awhile and survey the country around. It was wild and picturesque, and the sight of it was gratifying. We met a number of Indians. Their language and gesture were very strange, and they presented a most outlandish appearance. Many of them came into our camp with a variety of things to sell. When we returned, our camp was nearly deserted. The men had gone to the fort for equipments to commence our march. We hurried on, but only to be disappointed again. Too many companies were in before us. We went back to the camp, and spent the day quietly.

18th.—Every man was well fitted out with a musket and fifteen cartridges, a load of guns having been brought from the fort. I have now become accustomed to implicit obedience to orders—going and returning on errands to the fort—breaking mules, looking for strayed horses, cooking breakfast, washing clothes, &c. At night it rained hard, and while I tried to compose myself to sleep, I felt the shower dripping in my face.

20th.—The important morning had now arrived. It was the morning on which we were to "strike our tents and march away" for California. All was bustle and excitement, and we poor privates had to load the wagons with provisions for our long march. It fell to my lot as usual, to handle the bacon, pork, &c. And yet another trial awaited me: we had not travelled more than a mile, when we came to a deep slough or pond, through which I had to guide a mule. It was the first time I had the honour of leading a mule in gears. I had to dismount and wade through thick mud up to my waist. I had rather carried the mule on my back over a better road. What made the matter worse, I had my new clothes on, and they were almost ruined by the adventure. On stopping to encamp, a messmate kindly poured on water, while I washed the mud off, as well as I could, and laid down in my wet garments, very weary with my day's journey.

21st.—We are now fairly in the Indian country. The place assigned by the Government for the future residence of the tribes who have emigrated from the States. Here we found the prairies covered with grass—a seasonable supply for our horses, and a drove of ninety-five beeves, which we had brought out for present use. A strong guard was stationed around the encampment, at night, as roving bands of Indians were lurking around us, ready to seize any thing they could lay their hands on. We had travelled twelve miles when our captain thought it best to encamp for the night, as we found a little wood. The want of timber is a great defect in this otherwise beautiful country.

22nd.—We started this morning at 8 o'clock, and travelled fifteen miles through a lovely region, when we came to a settlement of the Delaware Indians. Their houses and plantations bear evident marks of civilization. In company with our first lieutenant, I called at a house, in the door of which sat two squaws making *moccasins*. Stretched on a bench nearby, lay an Indian fast asleep. He was a man of most powerful dimensions, at least six feet four, and fat withal. By his side rested a club full of notches. We did not care to disturb his repose, for we had slight misgivings that a notch or two more in that fatal war club, might record the finale of our own history.

We left him to his slumber, and hastened to the river, where we found several companies of our companions buying and selling among the squaws. Whiskey was the principal commodity, and a number of Indians were so much intoxicated that they could hardly tell a tree from a *moccasin*. The ferry is kept by the Indians. The Kansas River at this place is a bold stream; it was, nevertheless, safely passed by all, using boats only for our wagons; about sunset all landed, and we encamped about a mile from the river.

Sunday, 23rd.—Again we started on our journey. After the first ten miles of a broken country, some high hills appeared. They were very difficult of ascent, and we had much trouble with our teams. In two places we had to put our shoulders to the wheels. Orders were given that every man should secure what wood he could find, and we commenced packing it before us on our horses. A picturesque scene we must have presented, each man with his load of wood before him on his horse. While riding in this way we overtook Lieutenant Colonel Mitchell.

24th.—After passing a few clumps of trees, an immense prairie spread out before us, extending as far as the eye could reach. At 12 o'clock we came to a branch and encamped. The water here is in standing pools, and before drinking and making coffee, we were obliged to strain it through our handkerchiefs. While thus engaged, two Indians of the Sac Tribe made their appearance. They were elegantly mounted, but painted and tattooed in a frightful manner. They are smaller in stature than the Delawares, and at war with them. They called at our camp as a matter of curiosity. One of my mess, Levi Flowers, received a severe kick in his face from a horse, which nearly killed him. His face was much swollen.

25th.—The companies are now all united; having overtaken each other at different places. Our force was 1200 strong. We travelled all day in sight of trees like little dots on the horizon. At the end of our day's march we hoped to find water, *good* water, which our poor fellows needed after a long hot march, with nothing to protect their heads from the rays of the sun, but their glazed caps. The goal was reached. We rested beneath the shade of a small skirt of woods.

26th.—As usual, 8 o'clock found us ready to start. After a march of fourteen miles, we encamped on Beaver Creek We killed a beef; and the soldiers busied themselves in cooking supper. Not having conveniences of home at hand, we dispensed with our dinner daily- and satisfied ourselves with eating morning and night. Our captain is a good sort of man, and will no doubt do the best he can for us. And now while speaking of the captain, I will say a word or two about our lieutenants. Our first lieutenant, Mr. White, is nearly always in a good humour. He is large and somewhat corpulent—enjoys a laugh very much. He weighs 220lbs. net. Our second lieutenant, Mr. Smith, is of the middle size, very facetious, and always ready to accommodate. Our third lieutenant, Mr. Rock, was formerly a captain of Militia, but volunteering to go with the army to California, we elected him third lieutenant. He is a little over the middle size, and very reserved and stately.

27th.—After travelling twelve miles we reached the encampment of the Marion company, where we found a poor fellow who was accidentally shot last night, by a revolving pistol. Two men are left to take care of him. It is thought he cannot survive. Poor fellow! His fate is a sad one. Pursuing our journey, we passed Beaver Creek, and after travelling eighteen miles, came to the Big John River, where we encamped for the night.

28th.—The captain told us this morning that we should stop here for a day or two to rest ourselves. And now began a most ludicrous scene. Every camp kettle and other vessel that would hold water was brought in requisition, and the whole regiment commenced washing their clothes. To me it was a most singular sight. While rubbing away at our clothes a rumour reached us that we were on the route to Santa Fe, instead of California. This was news, and what with washing and what with talking we were kept pretty busy. On the route to Santa Fe, though we entered the journey for California. But alas! no matter where we are. We found our trip was not a "pleasure excursion," as many of our imaginations had so often pictured. The two soldiers we left, today have just come in, after digging the grave of their poor comrade.

29th.—This morning we caught some black trout and catfish in the Big John. They were very fine. Colonel Price had gone ahead, and at 12 o'clock we struck our tents, passed Council Grove, and encamped at 2 o'clock, a few miles further on, where there is a blacksmith shop, established by the government. Here I left letters for my friends in Maryland, to be carried back by the return mail to Fort Leavenworth.

Sunday, 30th.—Saw near the road, one of those singular mounds, of which I have so often read. It towered beautifully to the height of 100 feet. It may have been a mount of observation; it may be filled with the bones of the red men of the forest. I have no time, however, to speculate upon subjects so foreign from my present employment. At the end of 8 miles, we came to Rock Creek, and seven miles further we arrived at Diamond Spring, where we halted for the night.

31st.—This morning I filled my canteen with the refreshing water of Diamond Spring. At the Spring I counted forty-five wagons loaded with provisions for the army. Yesterday we entered upon the far-famed plains at Rock Creek. The scenery presents a dull monotony, a vast plain, almost level, bounded by the horizon, and covered with a thin sward and herbage.

September 1st.—Came to a place called the "Lost Spring," a most singular curiosity. The stream rises suddenly out of the ground, and after rushing over the sand a few yards, as suddenly sinks, and is no more seen.

2nd.—Today we are at the Cotton Wood Fork. It takes its name from a large cluster of cotton trees, the first I had seen after leaving Diamond Spring. There is a good stream of water here, and we enjoyed the blessing of a fine shower of rain. A little misunderstanding took place among the officers about starting. Some of them were too slow in their movements, and caused our captain to collect his men and make a speech. Several of the men were disgusted and became uproarious. A march of eight miles, however, to Turkey Creek, settled the question, and all appeared in pretty good humour.

Three miles further on, we came to Second Turkey Creek, nine miles beyond to Third Turkey Creek, and encamped. Turkey Creeks are plenty in this vicinity. How we would have rejoiced if the turkeys had been as plenty as the tides of the streams indicated. Third Turkey Creek is a lovely stream, running through the prairie. Here we wanted wood to cook with. As yet we had not seen any game, with the exception of two rabbits, caught by our men. They were of a novel species, almost white, with long black ears, and as large as a grey fox.

3rd.—About 12 o'clock today we came in sight of timber. Passed the Fourth Turkey Creek, and after travelling eighteen miles, encamped on the banks of the Little Arkansas, which at some seasons is a bold stream, with tremendous cliffs that can be seen at a long distance.

4th.—We are all huddled together in our tents, in consequence of a heavy storm of wind and rain, which came on last night. Some of the tents blew down, and most of the company were in a bad fix. Fires were necessary to keep us warm. We left at 8 o'clock, and after travelling ten miles, came to Owl Creek. Five miles from Owl Creek we reached Cow Creek, where we encamped. On the left we could see cliffs and timber at a great distance, and some small white spots like sand hills. On the right, nothing but a vast prairie. Just before we arrived at the Cow Creek, an antelope was started. Our boys gave chase and fired several times, but they missed him and he finally escaped. They must shoot better in fight with the enemy.

We had scarcely fixed up our tents, when the news came that a buffalo was in sight. In an instant, men on horseback, fully armed, were in pursuit from every direction. He was less fortunate than the antelope. The men had improved a little, and they overtook their game after a considerable chase, during which they fired fifty times. They killed him at last, and brought some of the flesh to the camp. It was of very little use, for with all our cooking, it was too tough to eat. He was a bull at least twenty years old. We had better let the old patriarch run.

Arkansas Bend, Saturday, 6th.—Here we stopped last night, after a most exciting day. Herds of buffalo were seen scattered over the plains. The best hunters were picked out to secure as many as possible. The chase was a fine one, thirteen were killed by the different companies. I strolled away from camp alone, to one of those mysterious mounds, which occur so frequently to the traveller among these wilds. On ascending it, I enjoyed a most magnificent prospect. It has the appearance of a fort, but when and for what purpose erected, will long remain a matter of uncertainty. I lingered so long that on my return

15

I found that my company had gone forward, but I soon overtook them.

Today we came to Walnut Creek, six miles from the mound. I felt stupid and sick; as I was placed on guard last night, on the banks of the Arkansas. I was all alone in the deep midnight, and I sat three long hours, with my musket, looking up and down the stream. I could see a great distance, as the sand on the shore is very white.

7th.—We were preparing to take a buffalo chase, when word was brought that the whole command must be moving. We were much disappointed, for we expected fine sport in the chase. On our route today, we passed Ash Creek, and five miles on came to Pawnee Fork. We saw herds of buffalo, and surrounded one, but they made a break towards the road, and crossed among the teams. They did no damage, however, nor was much damage done to them. I rode on briskly to overtake a friend, when my horse trod in a hole made by prairie dogs, (a small animal and very numerous here,) and fell with me. I received no injury except a little skin rubbed off my knee. On remounting, my attention was arrested by a horse running at full speed, and dragging something on the ground.

When he came closer, I discovered it to be a man whom his horse had thrown. The frightened animal stopped a little ahead of me, and I rode up, expecting to see a dead man, but as soon as his foot was extricated from the stirrup, to the surprise of all, he stood up and said that he was not much hurt. He said that he regretted most of all the loss of his clothes, which were torn in shreds from his body. Another man belonging to our company, by the name of Redwine, had a severe fall. He was taken into camp nearly dead. Chase was made again after buffalo, which appeared in thousands. Many antelopes also appeared, but it requires the fleetest horses to overtake them. Before we encamped we saw near the road side a little mound of stones, on one of which was engraved the name of R. T. Ross. It was supposed to be the grave of a man who was murdered by the Indians in 1840. He is resting in a lonely spot.

8th.—We are now on the banks of the great Arkansas river, after marching many miles through a barren and dreary looking country, almost destitute of grass or herbage. Here there is some improvement in this respect. A heavy rain caused our tents to leak, and drenched the poor soldiers, so that they passed a very uncomfortable night.

9th.—Kept up the river ten miles. A few scattered cotton trees, and cliffs, and sand banks are the only things to be seen. One of Col. Mitchell's men was near being killed today by an Indian. He had chased a buffalo two miles from camp, when an arrow was shot, which pierced his clothes; the poor fellow made all the haste he could to camp, with the arrow sticking in his pants. It was well it was not in his skin.

10th.—Last night, as soon as we were all snugly fixed, and ready for sleep, there arose a fearful storm of wind and rain, which gave our tents and ourselves a good shaking. Some of the tents were blown down, breaking in their fall the ridgepoles of others, and bringing them down also. In our tent, four of us held on with all our might, for nearly two hours, to keep it standing. Today we continued our march, travelling 15 miles, on the banks of the river. We saw a large flock of wild geese and tried to get a shot, but without success. They were too wild for us.

11th.—The weather was quite cold this morning, and there was so dense a fog as to prevent us from seeing a hundred yards ahead. There was an antelope killed today. The flesh tasted like mutton. We encamped by the side of the river, and an opportunity was afforded us of catching fish, which we accomplished by the novel mode of spearing them with the bayonet. Several dozens were caught, and we found them delicious.

12th.—Resumed our journey through the same scenery twelve miles; many antelopes were seen in herds, and prairie dogs barked at us in every direction.

Sunday, 13th.—As we proceed, the country assumes a still more dreary aspect, bare of verdure, and broken in ridges of sand. Our horses, enfeebled by their long travel, have very little to subsist on. The men, too, for the past three days, have ceased to receive rations of sugar and coffee. When we could not get these articles, we did as they do in France; that is, without them. We had to fry our meat, and a few of us entered upon the funny work of making soup out of pork, buffalo flesh, and fish, boiled up together. It was a rare mess, but we pronounced it first-rate.

14th.—After passing over the last fifteen miles today, we found ourselves at a place called the crossing of the Arkansas. We were then 362 miles from Fort Leavenworth. Our course has been along the margin of the river for 75 miles. At this place are steep bluffs difficult to descend. There are multitudes of fish in the river, many of them were killed by the horses' feet in crossing. We caught several varieties by spearing. A number of antelopes were killed here.

15th.—This morning I felt very dull from loss of rest. We had to give considerable attention to the cattle, horses, &c., to prevent them from straying. I and seven others were detailed to stand sentinel. I was appointed to the second watch, and to be in readiness at the hour, I spread my blanket down in the prairie to take a nap. In two hours I was awakened, and instructed to arouse the captain of the Watch at the expiration of three hours more; having no means to measure the time but by my own sad thoughts, and the weary hours being rather tardy, I too soon obeyed the orders, and kept the last watch on duty five hours, to the amusement of all.

After breakfast I took a stroll over the sand hills, and found about a dozen of our boys, inspecting the contents of a large basket, something like a hamper in which the merchants pack earthenware. It contained the skeleton of an Indian chief in a sitting posture, wrapped in buffalo robes, with his arrows, belts, beads, cooking utensils, &c. It had fallen from the limb of a tree, on which it had been suspended. Several of the men picked up the beads, and one named Waters carried the lower jaw and skull to camp, the latter he said he intended to "make a soup gourd of."

16th.—I took my seat quietly in the tent this morning, and thought I would rest, as we were to stay a day or two at this place. I was presently surrounded by soldiers begging me to write a few lines for them "to father, mother, wives, friends and homes." I wrote seven letters without removing from a kneeling posture, and was kept busy almost the whole day.

17th.—Our captain told us to get ready to start at 10 o'clock today, and as we were to cross a sandy desert sixty miles wide, much water and provisions were to be packed. A number of us were kept busy cleaning the salt from pork barrels in order to fill them with water. Scarcely had we finished this hard job, when the news spread like electricity, "that the mail from Fort Leavenworth had come in." I cannot pretend to describe the scene that ensued. I met our captain, who said "the Sergeant had a letter for me;" with the most peculiar feelings I seized it and saw the handwriting of my loved sister in Maryland; my home now so many weary leagues away. The delight I experienced was not unmmgled, however, with the thought that perhaps at this very spot, the entrance to a wild desert, I had bid *adieu* finally to all I held dear. We travelled twenty-two miles, and as it was late at it night when we halted, we spread our blankets on the sand, and slept soundly till morning.

18th.—I rose by daylight, and took a slice of bread and meat. We started early and came twenty-three miles, where we found some water standing in pools. We tried to erect the tents, but the wind was too high; had to cook that night with *buffalo chips*; strange fuel, even for soldiers to use.

19th.—After marching ten miles today, we came to the Cimarone Springs—a sweet stream. Here we found grass enough for our poor horses. It is truly an oasis m the desert.

Sunday, 20th.—We crossed an arm of the Cimarone, but the waters were dried up; dug for water, but found none. Went on five miles farther, dug again, and procured enough for ourselves and horses. In our route of twenty-five miles we saw the ground encrusted with salt. A singular animal attracted our notice. It was a horned frog, a great curiosity. Everything was involved in a thick cloud of dust.

21st.—One of the members of the Randolph Company, a gentleman by the name of Jones, died last night of consumption. He took the trip for his health, but today his remains were interred, not far from the camp, with the honours of war.

22nd.—We still travelled on the Cimarone, though only at certain places could we procure water. A deep sand retarded the progress of the army. On arriving where we had to encamp, we found 42 wagons, laden with goods. They were the property of a Mr. Gentry, a trader who has amassed great wealth, in merchandising between Independence, Santa Fe and Chihuahua. He speaks the Spanish language, and had nearly a dozen Spaniards in the caravan.

23rd.—We had a considerable storm last night, and the hard rain made it rather disagreeable, especially so to me, as I had to do the duty of sentinel in the first watch, with a wolf howling most dismally within sixty yards of me. I would have fired at him, but I had to obey orders and not arouse the camp by a false alarm. We saw today the bones of 91 mules, which perished in a snowstorm last winter. The bones were piled by the road side.

24th.—Overtook another caravan; still passing up the Cimarone, whose bed is through the sandy plain; at length we came to a hill from whence we descried the Rocky Mountains, rising abruptly in the distance. In our route we crossed a small spur. Mr. White, our first Lieutenant, with several others, ascended one, which presented the appearance of frowning rocky precipices. From its highest peaks, he brought down seashell, and petrifactions of various kinds. We had great difficulty in procuring buffalo chips. It was very amusing to see the boys in search of this indispensable article, our only resource to cook with.

26th.—We reached "Cool Spring" today, and found refreshing and delightful water, bursting from a solitary rock of enormous dimensions, the sides of which are covered with the names of various travellers. Our pleasant officer, Mr. White, called me up, saying "he wished to see my name on a spot he pointed out;" so taking a hearty draught from his canteen, which was just filled, I went up, and had scarcely carved my name, to remain there a monument of my folly, I suppose, when I discovered my horse making off with my accoutrements, canteen, &c. Hurried down and started after the beast. After running a great distance in the deep sand, I succeeded in capturing the runaway. Nineteen miles further on, we encamped in a deep ravine, among cliffs and rocks, here a few cedar trees were found. They afforded a seasonable supply of wood to cook with. The Rocky Mountains were in sight all day.

26th.—After a slight breakfast of bread and meat, we left this inhospitable place in disgust. It did not afford grass for our horses to graze on. We proceeded twelve miles through a dreary waste, and had to encamp at night in a place where there was no water.

27th,—I was awakened by the sergeant of the Guard at 2 o'clock this morning, it being my turn to stand sentinel of the morning watch. After breakfast we went on sixteen miles to Cotton Wood Creek. There we fixed up our tents, but no forage being found for our half-starved animals, we soon took them down again, and proceeded five miles on, to Rabbit Creek. At this place there was plenty of grass, and some tolerable scenery, but we were in no condition to enjoy it; being late in the night, we spread our blankets on the prairie, and composed our wearied limbs to rest.

28th.—Our journey was still continued through a dry and sterile land, where there is neither wood, water, nor grass; late in the evening we came to a pool of water. It was cool and good, and we drank of it freely. Our wagons did not come up till very late, and being tired, we wrapped ourselves in our blankets and laid down to sleep without supper. We went supperless, not to bed—but to the sod.

October 1st.—The last two days of September we remained at a place called Whetstone Creek, to rest. This Whetstone Creek is another oasis. It was the source of great joy to ourselves and our mules and horses. Our pastime was like the boy's holiday, whose mother allowed him to stay at home from school to saw wood and bring water. Our resting spell was a spell of hard work, and most industriously did we labour in cleansing our arms for inspection by the colonel. And we had to do a deal of marching and countermarching. Indeed the parade lasted so long, and with so many manoeuvres were we exercised, that the patience of officers and men was worn to its extremity. It was nearly threadbare. And then came the orders for every man to see to his own provisions and water, as another desert was to be traversed. So we go; changing from bad to worse. Today, after a march ten miles, we reached the "Point of Rocks;" a significant name. Late at night we encamped in a valley between high mountains, where there was some grass, but no water.

2nd.—We still moved on over barren rocks and sand hills. We laboured hard all day to leave them behind us. The hope cheered us of soon finding water; we realised it at the far-famed Red River. Our whole force encamped on its banks about nightfall. The waters of this distinguished river are brackish, but refreshing. Incrustations of salt are formed upon the rocks lying above its surface. This river was named Rio Colorado by the early Santa Fe traders, who, without having followed it down to any considerable distance, believed it to be the head waters of the great river of this name, which flows into the Mississippi below Natchez. It has, however, since been followed down to its junction with the Arkansas, and found to be the Canadian fork of that river.

We were now within 140 miles of Santa Fe, having marched more than 600 miles over a country destitute of timber, with but little water, and occupied only by roving bands of Indians, who subsist wholly upon buffalo meat. We saw immense herds of that animal on the Arkansas and its tributaries. The whole country presents, thus far, the most gloomy and fearful appearances to the weary traveller. But rough and uninviting as it is, all who visit New Mexico *via* Santa Fe, are compelled to pass it.

3rd.—We have journeyed well today, having reached St. Clair Springs. It is a beautiful spot, well watered, and glowing in delightful verdure. It is surrounded by mountains, the surface of which are covered with craggy rocks. We searched for miles around our camp for wood, with little success. The different companies killed a number of antelopes here.

Sunday, 4th.—We are still encamped, and shall remain in our position till the morning of the 5th. I took a walk, to "wagon mound," so called from the shape of its top, being like a covered wagon when seen in the distance. This mountain top is surrounded by a cliff of craggy rocks at least 100 feet in height. A most beautiful view is presented to the beholder. To the south you see hills covered with cedar and pine, situated in the immense prairie; to the north and north-west, are seen mountains with rocks piled upon rocks, with here and there groves of evergreens; far away to the east, is the desert, over which we had just passed.

The sides of this mountain are covered with a hard kind of sand, and pumice stone, having the appearance of cinder. Whilst I am writing, being situated as far up as it is prudent to go, an adventurous fellow, by the name of George Walton, has gained the wagon top; two others have also ascended; an achievement that few can perform. North of us there is a salt lake, which we intend to visit this evening.

Sunday Afternoon.—Lieut. Smith and myself took a stroll to the lake. We found a thick crust of salt around its edge, which is several miles in circumference. We returned to camp by a mountain path, very difficult to travel.

5th.—Eighteen miles were passed over today, through a mountainous country. We had just erected our tents and prepared for rest, when an evidence that we were approaching some civilised country, arrived in the shape of a Frenchman, who met us here with a travelling grocery. This concern came from Moras—a barrel of whiskey was strapped on the back of a poor mule, which stuff some of our soldiers were foolish enough to drink: it sells at $1 per pint. Such dear drinking ought to make drunkards scarce.

6th.—Saw a mud cottage on the road side today. The sight was most pleasant to our eyes, accustomed as they were for forty-four days to a wild waste. As we rode up, everyone must have a look into the house. It was inhabited by a native of North Carolina, whose wife is a Spanish woman. After being somewhat gratified with the sight of a house, though built of mud with its flat roof, we went on eighteen miles, and encamped at a town called Rio Gallenas Bagoes. On visiting this place we were struck with the singular appearance of the town and its inhabitants. The town consists of mud huts containing apartments built on the ground. The men were engaged in pounding cornstalks from which sugar is made; the women with faces tattooed and painted red, were making *tortillas*. We ate some, and found them excellent.

7th.—The wagons which contained our provisions coming in sight, we prepared the wood, which we obtained with difficulty, for boiling the coffee, &c., when Col. Mitchell rode up and told us the wind was too high to encamp. And hungry as we were, we went ahead seventeen miles through a forest of pine to Ledo Barnell, where we encamped for the night. A grisly bear was killed today by some members of the Randolph Company.

8th.—We passed the large village of San Miguel today. Col. Mitchell and his interpreter went forward in search of a good place to encamp. The weather was dry and pleasant, with a suitable temperature for travelling. The most disagreeable annoyance is the sand, which is very unpleasant when the wind is high.

9th.—Colonel Mitchell had chosen a spot for our encampment, about twelve miles from our last resting place, near the foot of a mountain. There was no water to be found. Impelled by necessity, we followed an Indian trail over the mountain five miles, and after riding through the thick pines for several hours, we found the coveted treasure. As may be supposed, we drank most heartily, after which we filled our canteens, and returned to camp about 12 o'clock at night. We learned that Santa Fe was about twenty-five miles off.

10th.—We arrived at the mountain pass at 10 o'clock, and reached Santa Fe about 3 o'clock in the afternoon. The glorious stars and stripes floating over the city was the first object that greeted our sight. We formed and marched into the town in order. We were received with martial music, and several rounds of blank cartridges were fired as a welcome to us. We paraded in the square fronting the Governor's house. After parade I took a walk through the town. The wagons did not arrive with our tents in time for us to encamp, and with our blankets around us, we laid down to rest. The blue sky was our canopy.

Sunday, 11th.—It was so cold and disagreeable last night, that I found it impossible to sleep. I shivered through the night on the hard soil, and rose this morning with a severe headache. I walked about to keep myself warm. After eating three small crackers for breakfast, I went to church in company with several others, to hear a Catholic priest. The music was prettily performed on various instruments. An old man in the meantime turning round before an image, and after he had bowed to the people several times, the music ceased.

All was over, and we returned to camp. I felt sick and sad, for the worship did not refresh my spirits. This evening I was pall-bearer to a member of the Benton Company, who died in the hospital soon after his arrival. We carried him out about a mile from the city to his final resting place. Four others were buried today, who died from fatigue and exhaustion. They belonged to the different companies. The muffled roll of the drum, and the firing of the farewell to the dead, did not have a tendency to cheer me.

12th.—This morning the roll was called, and various duties assigned the soldiers. Some had to work on the fort, and others to cut and haul wood. In the latter employment I had to become teacher to some green hands. I found the task very troublesome, but performed it to the best of my ability. In the evening I wrote letters to my friends in Maryland.

16th.—The two past days have been employed in preparations for our departure from Santa Fe. We have encountered much trouble and perplexity in getting teams, &c., have to travel eighty miles up the mountains, where we shall take up our winter quarters. We went out six miles and encamped. Having a severe headache, I tried my best to get some rest at night, but I had scarcely fallen asleep, when I was awakened by the officer to stand guard. I arose mechanically, feeling pretty much as I should suppose a fellow might feel who was on his way to execution. Taking up my gun I went to a large fire, where I sat quietly for two hours, watching my feelings more than I did the camp, for I was very unwell.

16th.—The breaking down of some wagons detained us here till late. After starting, we met a number of Spaniards, mounted on mules. We passed some little patches of corn, badly cultivated, which they dignify with the name of farms. A messmate wishing some red pepper,

I called with him at a house, but it was all "*no comprenda*"—"don't understand you," so we got no red pepper. We went on to the next habitation through a broken country; here we found our third lieutenant with the interpreter arranging for our camp. As we had to wait for the other companies to come up, I rested on some corn shucks, and very pleasantly did the bed feel. It was a bed of down in comparison with that to which I had been accustomed. I had slept on the ground for more than three months. Nothing grows spontaneously in this country, but the Spanish broom.

17th.—Colds, and other complaints, are becoming common in our ranks. After the fatigue of marching on foot heavily armed, we were illy calculated to do the duties of the camp. Our horses being too much enfeebled for further use, after our arrival at Santa Fe, were sent up the mountain to recruit. Thus our hardships increase with our progress. The ground being very broken where we encamped to-night, which is in a wheat field, I gathered all the stubble I could, to make our beds soft and even—bought some wood to cook with from the natives.

18th.—I started alone, and tried to overtake two messmates, who had gone on before me. I had not proceeded more than six miles when I found my two young gentlemen playing cards on the roadside. I passed them, and came to a village where I saw a considerable number of Spaniards. An old woman invited me in her house and set before me some *tortillas* and cornstalk-molasses, which were quite a treat. I remained there several hours, but thinking I had missed my way, I was about to take leave, with many thanks for their hospitality, when, to my great surprise and embarrassment, the old lady and her daughter most affectionately embraced me.

I suppose it was the custom among these simple hearted mountaineers, but of which I was quite ignorant. I was thankful for the meal my hostesses had provided for me, but the hugging was a luxury I did not anticipate, nor was I the least ambitious of having it repeated. I found my company without much difficulty. We went on and crossed the Rio Grande. In the first stream I got my feet wet; the second was too deep for wading, and I was kindly invited by our sergeant to mount behind him. We encamped there, having travelled twelve miles that day.

19th.—We were surrounded by the natives, who appeared friendly. When we came to the place where our horses were feeding, we learned from the soldiers in charge, that some of them had died, and that several had been stolen or had strayed away; mine, of course, was among the missing. While the others were preparing to mount, I shouldered my musket and walked on, in sand half a foot deep. The walk was exceedingly tiresome. I saw large quantities of wild geese on the Rio Grande. After marching eight miles we encamped.

20th.—All on horseback this morning in fine style, except myself and a few others equally unfortunate. We made the best use of our scrapers through the sand. After walking a while, we came to a house on the road side, the inhabitants of which, men, women, and children, came rushing out. We were at a loss to know what it meant, till we saw them surround a coloured man, (our surgeon's cook,) who proved a novel sight to them. The poor fellow was quite mortified at being made a show of on account of his colour. We went on eight miles and encamped among the Utah Indians. They are at war with the Navi-hoes, who have hunted them nearly down.

After supper I asked permission of our captain to accompany Mr. White, and several others to their encampment. Here, around a large fire sat an Indian chief with his squaws. After being introduced by our interpreter, a council was called. After some jabbering, a regular war-dance commenced. Their best warriors, equipped in full costume, and painted most hideously, in twenty different ways, danced furiously around a large fire, to the music of kettles and drums. It was a horrid din, in which mingled the war-whoop. We gazed with astonishment till its conclusion, when an old chief made a long speech. We then returned to our camp to meditate upon what we had seen and heard, and to wonder at the strangeness of character and habit exhibited by those poor creatures.

21st.—We were surrounded by the Indians before our breakfast was over. They came on to Abique, and encamped near us. There are several villages in this place. We arrived about two o'clock, and took up our quarters. The companies under Major Gilpin, which were sta-tioned there, and which we had been sent to relieve, were greatly worn and reduced with their long stay among the mountains. There was another dance at night in the Indian camp—being much tor-mented with sandburs, I did not go out. We had to eat our provisions half cooked, from the scarcity of wood. I and a messmate were forced to "hook" too small poles from a fodder crib, and when we returned to camp we found the companies on parade, and the Captain telling them the order of the next day.

22nd.—The whole command, *viz.* two companies from Col. Price's Regiment, consisting of about one hundred and eighty man, were obliged to remove today four miles further up the river, in order to obtain grass and fuel, this place being entirely destitute of either. At night, I went with our interpreter and third lieutenant to several houses, to buy mutton. While on our errand we met with some ladies; one of them had a dough face; all the rest were smeared with red, and to my fancy, not at all beautiful. We returned to camp without our mutton, and not a little disappointed.

23rd.—The country here is bare and sterile to a great degree, but there is an improvement with regard to fuel, which is so necessary at this season, in this mountainous country. I believe we are stationary at last. I was kept busy all day writing letters for the soldiers, many of whom very gladly do my washing and mending in return for this slight service. I had rather at any time write than cook and wash and mend clothes.

24th.—I felt sick today. I took cold from a severe drenching, while on duty as a sentinel last night. A heavy cold rain was falling the whole time. I strove to assist in making our camp as comfortable as possible, and in the evening dispatched two letters to Santa Fe, for my beloved friends in Maryland.

Sunday, 25th.—At daybreak this morning, a number of Mexicans came into camp; jabbering to themselves in a great rage about something. At first we could not ascertain the cause of their trouble, there being no interpreter present, and none of the soldiers knowing enough of the Spanish language to comprehend their meaning; soon, however, it was discovered that about sundown last evening, the captain of our company had caused the embankment of their mill and irrigating pond, to be broken, a short distance above camp, on the bank of the river, so as to prevent it from overflowing the bed of his tent. The water of course rushed out with great force, tearing the embankment down, and washing the earth away for a considerable distance, stopping their mill, and leaving many families destitute of water; all of which serious injuries, the captain seemed disinclined to repair. This behaviour of the captain met with but little favour from his men; to their honour be it spoken.

26th.—This morning our lieutenant went round the camp to get volunteers to repair the broken ditch. All seemed unwilling to do anything; some had their horses to find, others to cut and haul wood. The men had no idea of labouring gratuitously for the repair of a deed wantonly done by their captain. I with several others walked four miles up the river, with our axes, for the purpose of getting wood. We crossed the river several times, in the wildest and most out-of-the-way places, between high cragged mountains, which it was impossible to ascend. We returned to camp with our wagon loaded, though we encountered great difficulty in accomplishing it. We found there was a disagreeable misunderstanding among the officers respecting the embankment. The captain wished soldiers detailed for its repair, and the lieutenants thinking it an imposition on the poor fellows to stand in the mud to work such cold weather, without compensation.

28th.—We are now living in the midst of the greatest abundance of life's luxuries. As an evidence of our high living, I will transcribe our bill of fare for the week. It is as follows:

Monday.—Bread, beef, (tough as leather,) bean soup.

Tuesday.—Tough beef, bread, and bean soup.

Wednesday.—Bean soup, bread, and tough beef, and so on to the end of the week.

The greatest *harmony* prevails in camp, especially among the officers; the captain and first lieutenant are the greatest *friends* imaginable; they do everything in their power for the good of the company. They are the *bravest* and most *patriotic* officers in the regiment. In this lovely and fertile valley, encamped on the banks of the Rio Charma, we are enjoying all the *blessings* of life. We are charmed by the surpassing beauty of the Spanish ladies, and living in so much *harmony* with, each other, that we almost imagine the "garden of Eden" to have been again raised for our enjoyment; and then. Oh! heavens, what a luxury, amid these joys, to feel the delightful sensations produced by the gentle and graceful movements of a Spanish *louse*, as he journeys over one's body! The very thought of it makes me poetic, and I cannot resist the temptation of dedicating a line to the memory of moments so exquisite. How appropriate are the words of Moore to such occasions of bliss?

Oft in the stilly night,
Ere slumber's chains have bound me,
I feel the cursed creatures bite,

As scores are crawling round me,
O not like one who treads alone,
The banquet halls deserted;—
In crowds they crawl despite the groan
Of him whose blood they started.

When I took up my *Journal* to add a few items, I found the above had been written by some wag, in my absence. He was disposed to ridicule my description of the felicity of which I boasted. Our boys are rather mischievous, and I must confess that I felt rather waggish myself, when I made the boast of our possessing Eden-like pleasures. The continuation of my narrative pleased me so well that I consented to let it remain as it was written. Our mischievous feeling and manner of expression is the most innocent way in which we can relieve ourselves, for we privates are suffering many privations, while some of our officers refuse to speak to each other. I am glad, however, that our troubles are so merrily turned into ridicule; the best way sometimes to treat them.

We are not destitute of sport, however; many amusing scenes occur among us, debating societies are formed among the soldiers, in which the most absurd questions are dilated upon with a vehemence and mock seriousness truly laughable. A breakfast of coffee, without sugar, some very poor beef soup, and onions sliced up with parched corn, made a better meal for us today, than we have had for some days past. Yesterday I traded off *two needles* to the Spanish girls for six ears of corn and some onions. It was a trade decidedly profitable for both parties. In company with our first lieutenant, his brother, William White, Dr. Dunlap, and a number of others, I went up on a high peak of the Rocky Mountains.

We had been there but a few minutes when it commenced snowing. We kindled a large fire, and amused ourselves by listening to the reverberations of sound produced by our lieutenant's revolver, who fired six rounds. Becoming thirsty, we searched and found water, in the crevice of the rock, close to the edge of the precipice. It was too far below the surface for us to drink by stooping over, and William White proposed to throw in gravel, in order to raise the water, reminding me of one of *Æsop's fables*. We followed his advice, and the water was soon forced to rise high enough for our purpose.

The snow increasing, we came down and made another fire in a large hollow of the rock, where all but myself sat down to cards. It was an amusement that I did not relish, and I sought my own gratification in loosing the rocks and rolling them down the side of the mountain, which is at least a thousand feet above the level of our camp.

29th.—Today, Charles Perkins and myself took our guns and proceeded down the river several miles in search of game. We fired at several flocks of wild geese and ducks, but it only scared them further off. We passed several Spanish houses on our return. When we reached the camp, we found the soldiers at different employments, some playing cards, and others making articles to sell to the natives. A Mr. Hatfield was engaged in the manufacture of a *grindstone* to trade to the Spaniards for corn and beans. These, with onions, are the only vegetables they grow.

30th.—The mountains are covered with snow, and, after raining hard all night, this morning it is clear and cold. We made the best preparations we could to send the wagons back to Santa Fe for provisions, as late last night, our second lieutenant returned, after an absence of five days, and brought news that we are to take up our winter quarters in this dreadful region. There seems to be very little likelihood of our going south at all. The officers went in search of other quarters today.

31st.—We had a heavy fall of rain last night, which improved into a snow storm before morning. I slept very uncomfortably, as a high wind from the north had full sweep in the door of our tent. We were inspected at 11 o'clock, and carried through all the evolutions of the drill. After the parade we could scarcely keep warm, though wrapped in our blankets, and crowded around the fire. Yesterday one of our beef cattle died from starvation. The Mexicans came down and took it off to their habitations. We might have made a speculation by selling it, but did not think of it.

Sunday, November 1st.—Several of my mess are going up the mountains to look for their horses. I offered a friend $5, (should I ever again possess that sum,) to search for mine. I read aloud in my Testament to some of the boys, while others sat apart or pitched quoits. At night a Spaniard came in camp with a fiddle, and played a number of tunes, which so exhilarated my poor half frozen companions, that they united in a dance, which they kept up till a late hour.

2nd.—Some *Taos* flour, coarsely ground in the little native mills on the Rio Grande, badly baked in the ashes, and some coffee without sugar, now comprise our only sustenance. Between meals, however, we parch some corn, which we now and then procure of the natives in exchange for buttons, needles, or any little matter we can spare. At 9 o'clock, we struck our tents, and marched down the river two miles, to a deserted Spanish house, nearly in ruins.

The inhabitants were murdered by the Navihoe Indians. This is the place where we are to take up our winter quarters, I can scarcely describe this wretched den. The soldiers have looked in and they have become very dissatisfied. They were told by the Captain to erect their tents inside the wall, all the houses in this region having that protection. We could not sleep in the house on account of the offensive odour. The tent was much more comfortable.

3rd.—As soon as our breakfast of beef soup and coffee was over, some of the men were appointed to scrape and clean the house. I, with several others, was sent to the mountains to cut and haul wood. After walking two miles, we procured a load of green pine, which does not grow here more than half the usual size. On the return, I thought I would take a near cut to our camp alone. I turned into a footpath, which led me to the top of a high mountain. Here I could see our quarters, though a long distance off. I took a direct course, and soon arrived at camp, where I found our boys writing down a vocabulary of Spanish words. They have become very erudite of late.

4th.—All this day we did nothing but write down words from the language spoken by the people, who, from their complexion, appear to be a mixture of the Spanish and Indian races. We made a pretty good dictionary among us.

5th.—This day is very unpleasant. It is raining hard. At 4 o'clock, our first lieutenant, Mr. White, returned from Santa Fe. He brought bad news. He could get no provisions, except one fourth rations of flour, and one and a half barrels of mess pork. But notwithstanding all this, our boys are still very lively.

6th.— We had great labour today in procuring fuel sufficient for our present purpose, and the prospect of a long and severe winter before us, makes our situation rather unenviable.

7th.—On short allowance yesterday and today, a little bread, (*i.e.* two pints for six men,) some fried bee , and coffee without sugar.

Sunday, 8th.—Although the morning was cloudy and cold, I walked with twenty others down to Abique to church. On arriving we went into the priest's room. He very politely invited us to be seated, and then commenced asking all kinds of questions about the United States. He seemed to take great interest in teaching us the Spanish language. He made us repeat after him, many long and hard words.

We sat two hours with him, and then went to church, where a large congregation was assembled. In a few minutes our priest made his appearance, dressed in gold lace, and ascended the pulpit, while all present fell on their knees. The music of various instruments now commenced, the priest the meanwhile drinking sundry glasses of wine. The people remained on their knees till the music ceased, when all retired.

It was noised among the soldiers that a *fandango* would take place in the evening. Some of us went in to inquire of the priest, who informed us that the fandango was to be at a village a few miles further off. In a little while a Mexican guide was hired to escort us. After walking a mile we came to a river, when this Spanish fellow, very quietly sat down to pull off his shoes, and told all who were in favour of wading the stream to follow his example. Eight of the boys immediately commenced stripping to cross, declaring that nothing should disappoint them from attending a fandango. As I had a bad cold, with some others, who felt no inclination to wet their feet, I returned to our quarters.

9th.—All this day in the mountains, cutting wood.

10th.—I went with several others to search for lost horses. We had not gone far, when, to my great joy, I found mine, which had not been seen since we left Santa Fe. We heard volleys of musketry in the direction of our camp, and were at a loss to understand the meaning, till on our return, we learned that a dog had been buried with the honours of war. This poor dog had been a great favourite with our captain and all the company; he was most foolishly shot by a soldier on guard last night. The man was made to dig his grave, and will be detailed on extra duty as a punishment, the captain being much exasperated. This evening I, with four others took rations for five days, in order to drive the horses down the river to graze.

Late at night, we reached a Spanish village, where we stopped. A mile from that place, a *fandango* was to come off, and the ladies of the place were preparing for the dance. They were nicely equipped in their best finery, and the soldiers were engaged to accompany them.

Not being very desirous of attending the *fandango*, I preferred to remain and try to get some rest, of which I was very much in need. The party was soon prepared, and off they started, leaving me behind to cook supper and arrange matters for their comfort when they should return. I browned the coffee, fried the beef, made the bread, and having all things in readiness, I drank a cup of coffee and laid down to rest on a mattress placed on the floor.

As far as the thing I laid on was concerned, I was comfortable enough; the mattress was a luxury; but I could not sleep; the reasons were various. I was lying in a house, when I was accustomed to dwell in tents;—my quarters were divided between myself several donkeys and mules and two small children—the odour of the donkeys was not the most agreeable, nor their noise very harmonious; the children knew their mother was out, and did their best at crying. The woman had gone to the *fandango*, where I hope she enjoyed better music than that which she left for the lulling of my sensibilities into sweet slumbers.

11th.—Our soldiers did not return from the *fandango* till 3 o'clock this morning, and I was appointed to get breakfast while they slept. I had considerable trouble in accomplishing this service, as the girls crowded around the fire, and I had frequently to pass the frying pan over the naked feet of a pretty girl who was sitting near me. In company with a young Spaniard, who was exceedingly agreeable and polite, I went out after breakfast to kill wild geese. We walked a long distance, and returned unsuccessful.

*12th—*I find the family residing here, very agreeable. I was invited, and almost forced to accompany them to a *fandango* last night (for they do little else but dance.) All on horseback, the married men mounted behind their wives, we started. A little baby in its mother's arms becoming troublesome, one of our men, who said he was a married man, most gallantly rode up, and offered to carry the little creature. The mother thankfully resigned it to his charge. There was more pleasure in the idea of enjoyment at the *fandango* than in taking care of a cross child. When we arrived at Abique, an old man invited us to partake of his hospitality;—an invitation we gladly accepted. We went in accordingly, and after all were seated on the floor in the posture of a tailor, a large earthen vessel was placed before us containing pepper sauce and soup, and a few *tortillas*, (a thin paste made of corn rubbed between flat stones.) The sauce caused my mouth to burn to a blister.

The people are very fond of condiments, and become so accustomed to them that what will burn a stranger's mouth has no effect upon theirs. After all was over, we went across the street to attend the fandango. From the crowd, I should judge it was high in favour with all classes of the community. Some of the performers were dressed in the most fantastic style, and some scarcely dressed at all. The ladies and gentlemen whirled around with a rapidity quite painful to behold, and the music pealed in deafening sounds. I took my seat near a pretty girl, and every time she leaned on my shoulder, which she did pretty often, her beau would shake his head in token of his displeasure, and showing his jealous disposition, I left the place about 10 o'clock, and returned to our quarters.

13th.—We visited our camp today at the Spanish ruins. The captain and officers were glad to see us, especially as we had good news in relation to the horses. We had them in charge, and exhibited them to our comrades as the trophies of our success. On our return, we killed two wild geese and four rabbits, which we found a great help to our stock of provisions, which was then very low.

14th.—I was left alone with the Spaniards today, while our boys are attending to the horses. My Spanish friends are very courteous, but there is little to relieve the monotony of our intercourse, as from my ignorance of the language, I am unable to converse with them.

15th.—This morning we had one of our wild geese stewed for breakfast, which we had without coffee, and almost without bread. After breakfast I started to camp, to draw provisions of some kind. When at camp, I concluded to remain there.

16th.—I was told by the sergeant today, that there was no flour to issue. He referred me to the captain, who directed young Bales and myself to a mill some distance off, where we procured 60lbs. of unsifted *Taos* flour, very coarsely prepared. With this we returned, and in a few minutes nearly the whole was appropriated to the use of the half-starved soldiers. A very small portion of this brown flour fell to our share. This evening we are without food, or nearly so. Martin Glaze, an old veteran, who has seen service, and belongs to my mess, got a few ears of corn, and parched it in a pan, with a small piece of pork, to make it greasy. When it was done, we all sat round the fire and ate our supper of parched corn, greased with fat pork. The weather tonight is extremely cold.

17th.—Awoke early this morning and found it snowing very hard. At 10 o'clock I went to our first lieutenant's quarters. He was engaged in appraising some cattle which are pressed into our service, and for which the natives were to be paid. A bull has just been killed, and the offals are being greedily devoured by our poor fellows. At 11 o'clock today our third corporal died, having been sick with camp fever and inflammation of the brain, several weeks. At 3 o'clock his grave was dug, and the poor fellow was wrapped in his blanket, and buried without a coffin. Tonight there are several of our men sick with the measles, supposed by our surgeon to have been brought from Santa Fe.

18th.—The snow four inches deep—clear and very cold—another grave dug today, for a member of the Livingston company, making five who have died since we have been out here. They are all buried near the mountain, where poor Johnson was laid.

20th.—The past two days have been employed in procuring wood, which is hard labour; but we do not complain as our fare is improved by the addition of bean soup and coffee.

21st.—A court martial was held this morning to try our fourth sergeant, who has said something derogatory to the character of our orderly. After the court adjourned, we were ordered to form a line. Our first lieutenant then stood in front and read the proceedings of the court. The decision was, that our fourth sergeant be reduced to the ranks, for slander. It was ordered, that if any man or men should thereafter bring false charges against the officers, he or they should be sent with a file of soldiers to Santa Fe, and tried at headquarters, &c. The company was then dismissed. Several of my mess concluded to run as candidates for the vacant place. They went among the crowd with tobacco and parched corn, electioneering. I was placed a guard at 9, and had to stand till 11 o'clock.

Sunday, 22nd.—A gloomy Sabbath morning; I felt badly, but concluded to go to church at Abique. As soon as the ceremonies were ended, I went to the priest's room, in company with my old friend, Capt. Markle, and several officers. After sitting a while, a servant brought in a dish of refreshments, consisting of pies and wine. Placing the glass to my lips, I discovered it to be Taos whiskey, as strong as alcohol. A piece of the pie, I thought, might take away the unpleasant taste, so I crowded my mouth full, and found, alas! it was composed of onions; a dreadful fix, indeed, for a hungry man, Taos whiskey and onion pie!

the very thought of the mess makes my mouth burn. When I returned to camp, I found nearly every individual busily engaged at cards Elias Barber, a messmate, was taken sick with the measles. The disease is now raging among the troops.

23rd.—We had great trouble in procuring fuel today. We had to travel far up the mountain for it, and it is exceedingly difficult to cook with it out of doors in the deep snow. It fell to my lot to make the bread, and I had much ado tonight, to make the mass stick together. I felt more than usual fatigue after the parade.

24th.—Elias Barber is very sick today. He spent a wretched night last night in a thin cotton tent. The wind is blowing on him constantly, while the measles are out very thick. I went to the captain this morning and informed him of the situation of the young man. He told me if I could procure a place in the house, he might be brought in. I therefore went and after making preparations to move him, I was told that no such thing should be done. I then tried to get an extra tent to place over the one we are sleeping in, and even this was denied me. The poor fellow is lying out of doors, exposed to all the inclemency of this cold climate. And last night it was so cold that the water became frozen in our canteens. The surgeon appears interested, but it is all to no purpose—nothing further is done for the comfort of the sufferer. May the Lord deliver me from the tender mercies of such men!

25th.—I felt quite unwell all day today. I suffered much from a severe attack of diarrhoea. Our lodgings are very uncomfortable. I went down to the Rio Grande to get water, and found it nearly frozen over. A great mortality prevails among the troops who are dying from exposure and disease.

26th.—I was very much engaged all day, in nursing poor Barber. He is worse today, the measles having disappeared from the surface. I sat by him the livelong night and listened to his delirious ravings, and I felt sad to think I had no means of relief At 4 o'clock this morning the captain came, and finding him so ill, brought out a tent to cover the one he laid in.

27th.—Last night, my messmate Phillips returned from Sante Fe, with a message from Col. Price to the different captains, to send on ten men from each company, as an escort for Col. Mitchell, who was about to start for Chihuahua. From thence he is to proceed to open a communication with General Wool. Today an express arrived from

Col. Mitchell for the same purpose. We were hastily paraded to ascertain how many would volunteer to go, when I, with live others of my company, stepped out of the ranks, and had our names enrolled. We were satisfied that we could not render our situation worse, and hoped any change might be for the better. We hastened to the grazing ground, over the mountain, for our horses, which occupied us all day. Mine was gone of course. To prevent delay, I gave my note to a young man for a horse which belonged to a deceased soldier.

28th.—A full company having been made up, this morning we gathered at our quarters, and were ready at 8 o'clock to take leave of our kind hearted comrades. They bid us "goodbye," with many expressions of regret, and injunctions to write often. We pursued our journey thirty-five miles, and put up late in the evening at the house of a rich Spaniard, who accommodated us with an empty room twenty feet square, but it had so small a fireplace that we could not use it for our culinary purposes, so we were forced to do most of our cooking in the open air. It fell to my lot as usual to make the bread, and I kneaded forty pounds of Taos flour in a mass, and baked thirty- six good sized cakes, while two others prepared our camp kettles of coffee, &c.

Sunday 29th.— At 4 o'clock we ate our breakfast, and were on the road by daylight. We travelled all day without stopping, and arrived at Santa Fe at 6 o'clock in the evening. We went immediately to the American Hotel where supper was provided for us. Nineteen men sat down to the table, none of whom had enjoyed such a privilege for nearly four months. All were hungry, and it was amusing to see how we tried to eat our landlord out of house and home. After supper we retired to our quarters in a very small room.

30th.—Word was sent from Col. Mitchell this morning for us to parade before the Governor's house for inspection. Our horses were also examined, and all being found in good order for the trip, we were dismissed and conducted to our quarters, in the court house, where we drew our rations, *viz.* thirty pounds of good American flour, with pork enough to last five days.

December 1st.—Paraded soon again after breakfast, and were told by our captain that previous to our departure, we must all march to the sutler's store, and acknowledge our indebtedness to him; so we rode up in right order, and dismounted. We had a peep at our accounts, and

I found mine to be $30.75. I had purchased a few articles of clothing on my route, being forced to do so from necessity. I was, therefore, not surprised at the amount, especially when I read the prices of some of the articles, *viz.* a small cotton handkerchief, $1; suspenders, $1; flannel shirt, $3; tin coffee pot, $1.60, &c., &c. Here we bade farewell to our captains, who had accompanied us to Santa Fe to see us off. Captain Williams shook me cordially by the hand, saying he had no expectation of seeing me again in this world.

Captain Hudson now took charge, and rode with us two miles out of town; here he informed us we had a dangerous road to travel, but would leave us to the care of Lieutenant Todd for two days, till we were joined by Colonel Mitchell and himself He returned to town, and we came on four miles and stopped at a house, whose master sold us wood and forage for our horses, it being severely cold. Sixty of us occupied two large rooms for the night.

2nd.—We marched twenty-five miles to a place called San Domingo, and took quarters in a deserted house. This is a considerable place, with a handsome church, which was being illuminated when we arrived. In a little time the bells began to ring, and there was a firing of musketry and considerable commotion at the door of the church. Several of our soldiers were induced to go up and inquire into the meaning of the uproar. We were told that a converted Indian chief had just died, and that all this was to prevent him from going down to purgatory. The roll of the drum, and firing, continued a long time, when the ceremonies commenced in the church, from the door of which we saw many large wax candles burning, but not being permitted to enter, we very quietly retired.

3rd.—After travelling six miles we came to an Indian village, called San Felippe, and two miles further down the Rio Grande, we encamped in the midst of a good pasture for our horses. After supper our lieutenant told me I was honoured with the appointment of captain of the watch. In consequence of this distinction, I had to be up nearly all night. It was very cold. We were now comparatively happy, for we had plenty of good flour from the States, with coffee, sugar, &c.

4th.—We learn that we shall be obliged to stay here till Colonel Mitchell comes up with the other company, so we seize the opportunity to have our horses shod. Two blacksmiths are now at work; I have just bought a set of shoes and nails from our sutler, for $3.

5th.—The weather has moderated somewhat, but the face of the country presents nothing inviting at this season of the year. Everything has a desolate and wintry appearance. There being no food for our horses, we chopped down some limbs of the cotton wood tree for them to eat. Then went to a Mexican village to buy corn. Having no money, I took some tobacco and buttons to trade for the corn. While here, I sold my greasy blanket for a Navihoe one, with a meal for my horse in the bargain. The man with whom I traded was very kind; he set before me some corn, mush and sausages, but being seasoned with onions, I declined eating. He then brought in some cornstalk molasses, which I mixed with water and drank, thanking him for his hospitality. I returned to camp, where I found that Col. Mitchell and the baggage wagons had arrived. I was officer of the guard tonight, and up till 12 o'clock.

Sunday, 6th.—Formed in line by our colonel, in the midst of a heavy shower of rain, and marched down the Rio Grande, a long distance. Our course is due south, keeping the river constantly on our right, and ranges of mountains on our left hand. We passed many villages, and at night encamped near one.

7th.—Rising early this morning to prepare breakfast, I found the snow four inches deep, and still snowing very fast. Marched in right order fifteen miles, and after passing several towns situated on the banks of the river, we stopped at night at the large town of Albikirk. Here are garrisoned one hundred and fifty regulars, near whose quarters we encamped in a large room 100 feet by 40. In this place we found a number of soldiers, some engaged in tailoring, some playing cards, and others amusing themselves in various ways.

8th.—The country through which we passed today is thickly dotted over with towns and villages, whose names I cannot remember, but the road is dismal enough, being still among the mountains, where every object the eye rests upon is covered with snow. The cold is very intense. We pitched our tents tonight under the walls of a town. We had six small ears of corn for our horses, and no fodder. I went to the quarter master and was informed by him that the Mexicans had refused to sell us anything. I cut some buttons from a uniform jacket, and with them tried to purchase food for my horse, but I was refused everywhere. I sat down and made out a requisition, and with several others went to their large stacks, ten feet high, which we ascended, and threw down a large turn for each. We succeeded in coming off with our booty, and in a few minutes, we were in bed. We were not disturbed in conscience in the least, being fully covered by the axiom, "necessity knows no law."

9th.—We were called up this morning to lead our horses into ranks, when two guns and a sabre were missing. They had been taken from the tents by the Mexicans. After the line was formed. Col. Mitchell ordered the men who had lost their arms, to march out. He then told them they would be left behind to search the town, assisted by the *alcade*, and if they should not find their arms they would have to return to Santa Fe. We then left: marched ten miles and encamped near a village. Our interpreter was sent to procure forage for the horses, but he returned with the news that none could be had.

Our captain told the sergeant to go up with a file of soldiers and *take* what was wanting. He formed a line of twenty men, I among them, and marched off with our orderly at the head, and second sergeant, with the bags to put the corn in. At the door of the house, we were ordered to halt. The lock was broken, and we entered, filled our sacks and packed them down to the camp. In this adventure I made the acquaintance of a young man by the name of Hepbourn. He was born and raised in Prince George's County, Md. After supper, we were all ordered up to draw fifteen rounds of cartridges. A strong guard was ordered out tonight.

10th.—Having orders to march very early, we rose by light and proceeded down the river eighteen miles, the country presenting very much the appearance already described. We saw a few vineyards, surrounded by walls. I felt miserably disordered from the cold and loss of rest. I was just about to sit down to supper, which I thought might revive me, when our orderly came by, requesting the men to form in line immediately, as the captain wished to read the *Articles of War*. We stood just one hour and listened to the dry detail. When the reading was concluded, we returned to our tents. After supper, sixteen men were detailed on guard. I stood two hours the first watch, and three hours before daylight. It was extremely cold.

11th.—The roll was called at daybreak, and after parade we continued our march twelve miles, and encamped in a town among the mountains. Wood was very scarce, and the severity of the weather increasing.

12th.—We eat our breakfast at daylight. It consisted of mess pork and bread, half baked by a miserable fire. We went twelve miles to a place where there is a fine supply of wood. Our poor fellows had the satisfaction of having a good fire all night, and it was very necessary, for the weather was tempestuous with cold gusts of wind and snow.

Sunday 13th.—At one o'clock this morning I awoke and found myself so cold that I arose and went to the guard fire to thaw myself. I stood by the fire till daylight. The captain in his round to visit the guard, stopped at the fire, and I had a pleasant chat with him.

He is very clever and condescending. He remained an hour or two, and then woke up the orderly to have all in readiness for a start. We came over the mountain four miles, where our road intersected the river again, passed a town, and further on encamped near the river. Our interpreter bought a beef from the natives, also a little wood to cook it. The wild geese are very numerous here.

14th.—The roll was called very early this morning—and as my horse had a sore back, I asked the captain's permission to walk behind the wagons. I walked all his day and led my horse. When I came up to the encampment I found that my mess had supper ready. It consisted of a kind of chicken pie, bread and coffee. I relished the supper very much, but by way of dessert I received information that I had to stand sentinel. I walked my post two hours and then went to bed; being too cold to sleep, I got up at two o'clock, and went to the guard fire. The guard said he was very sleepy and would lie down if I would consent to serve while he slept. To this I readily agreed—and he laid down, while I made a large fire, which soon attracted the attention of the other sentinels, and several of them collected around it. We enjoyed each other's conversation till the morning dawned.

15th.—I woke up the sergeant, who said we had walked our post four hours over the time. I received the compliment, but did not tell him that we had sat by the fire all the time. In his Irish brogue, and with a pipe in his mouth, he proceeded to call the roll. We are to stay here till the 17th.

16th.—Having secured some beef, I made a large fire to get an early breakfast. Yesterday our quarter master pressed a lot of seven very good cattle from the Mexicans. Last night a strong guard of twenty men was stationed around our camp. The weather is still raw and cold. We are yet among the mountains.

17th.—This morning we reached the *second crossing* of the Rio

Grande. Four miles beyond the crossing, we overtook Col. Doniphan's command, and encamped near them. Having to walk and lead my horse, I did not come up till all were fixed. I found our boys very angry at a circumstance which they related and made me write down, with a promise to publish it—which promise I now fulfil.

While on the march today, the captain ordered a halt, and told the soldiers that he had been requested by the lieutenants to beg them all not to come near their fires or tents, as it incommoded them greatly. He stated on his own behalf, as well as on behalf of the other officers, that it was quite a nuisance to have the privates lurking about their tents and fires. He said that something might be "hooked" and that the lieutenant had already lost some *saleratus*, &c. This was a poser. Our poor fellows could hardly endure it. Some of them were much exasperated. I tried to soothe them, and told them no other harm was meant than a slight intimation that we must keep away at meal times, as a knowledge of their better fare might make us dissatisfied, &c. All passed off better than I expected. We had to go a mile for water, and the thermometer at zero.

18th.—The situation of our tents was by no means pleasant. There was much complaint about stones and hillocks, lying hard, &c. Breakfast over, I started with the wagons, in company with some others, whose horses' backs were sore. I felt stupefied from the cold and loss of rest, having walked my round five hours last night. We went on twelve miles, which we trudged on foot. At night we cut some branches of the cotton wood for our horses to eat. We were preparing to rest, when our captain told us, if any man lost his horse he would have to walk back to Santa Fe. He further said, that we had to go through a gloomy region or desert, 85 miles in extent, where no wood or water could be procured. He' advised us to go to work and prepare food enough to last three or four days. I made up 30 lbs. of flour and baked eighteen cakes, while the balance was attended to by my mess.

19th.—We were all busy providing against the perils of our difficult and dangerous march. We shall have to keep close company, as the Navihoe Indians roam this desert in bands. At 11 o'clock we moved off in fine order, and marched fifteen miles over the dreary plain. At 3 o'clock at night the Captain ordered a halt. We picked up a few weeds, kindled a little fire, took a cold cut of bread and meat, and laid on the ground to rest, without erecting tents. A young man having drank too much of the "*ardiente*," very unluckily offended one of the officers, and was ordered to be tied to the wagon wheel. He cut a variety of capers while this was being done. His friends soon set him at liberty.

20th.—The news of a "spring in the desert" was brought by some scouts, who had started out on an exploring expedition. They found the spring in a place full six miles from our road. We drove the cattle over a miserably rough path to drink from the spring, which turned out to be a muddy pool. We afterwards marched fifteen miles and encamped late at night. We took a slice of bread and meat, and laid down to rest on our blankets.

21st.—The appearance of our captain very early this morning, aroused us. He came with the intelligence that Major Gilpin had sent on an express last night for a reinforcement, as he was expecting an attack every moment, from the enemy. In a few minutes we were on the march, and without stopping to take breakfast, we travelled thirty-five miles. We encamped late at night, three miles from the river, where men and beasts, thirsty and weary, were refreshed, I was afraid my horse would kill himself drinking. With six others, I pressed some oxen from the traders, whom we found encamped here, as most of our teams had given out, and were left upon the road.

22nd.—Passed over fourteen miles of broken, wretched country today, the soil of which produces nothing but a kind of shrub called soap-weed. The inhabitants, it is said, use this weed in washing their clothes. We encamped in a rough place, among stones and hillocks.

23rd.—I trust the end of this "*jornada*," as it is called, and which means the "region of death," is nearly reached, for a march of twelve miles brought us to a village, where we halted to take in provisions brought by our quarter master. Proceeding two miles further, we came up to Major Gilpin, whom we found encamped on a large sandy plain. We had to go two or three miles for wood. Our flour was nearly gone, and we had a little beef soup and rice for supper at night. The boys being still hungry, we went to the village and procured some dried fruit and pumpkins, which we sliced up and stewed in our camp kettles. Of this fare we partook heartily, and laid down to sleep in the sand.

24th.—The first blast of the bugle this morning made us hurry into line. Some of the men being rather tardy, were too late, and they were told by the officer who inspected us, that any man who did not come into rank at the sound of the bugle, would be made to stand guard three days. We broke ranks and ate our breakfast, which consisted of a small piece of bread, made up with pumpkin. The weather is now quite pleasant, and the country, hitherto so uniformly desolate, begins to improve in appearance.

BATTLE OF BRACITO.

26th.—In the union of our forces we are one thousand strong. Moved as early as usual from the position we have occupied the last three days, and after marching twelve miles, we came to Bracito, and encamped as 10 o'clock. We stripped our horses as usual, and picketed them out, went to hunt wood to cook our dinners. Some of the men had gone at least a mile from camp, when the alarm was given, "*to arms! to arms!*" Looking in the direction pointed out, we saw a cloud of dust, as if the whole of Mexico was coming down upon us. Unwilling to throw away our wood, we ran with our turns on our shoulders, when we heard an officer hallooing, "Throw away your wood, and bring your horses into camp." We obeyed the order as quickly as possible.

We found our orderly at his post, directing the men to load their guns and get into line. Every man was at his proper places in a few minutes. By this time the Mexican army was in sight, and had formed in battle array at a distance of a mile from us. Presently an officer came out of their ranks, handsomely mounted, and bearing a black flag. Colonel Milchell, accompanied with the interpreter, rode up to meet him on half-way ground, to inquire his business. He told them he had come to demand the surrender of our entire force, by submitting, he said our lives would be spared; if we did not, every man would be put to death.

Our interpreter cut short his harangue, by telling him to "go to hell and bring on his forces." In the meantime our company, (the Chihuahua Rangers,) received orders from head quarters, to right about face, and march from the right, where we were somewhat protected by brush, weeds, and gopher hills, to the extreme left, in open ground, to withstand the charge of the Mexican cavalry, so off we marched in double quick time, to our position on the left. Our captain here told us to reserve our fire till the enemy was in fair rifle distance, and added that he hoped no man in his command would act the coward, but all would do their duty as volunteers and American soldiers. He had scarcely done speaking, when the enemy commenced firing at us, from three to four hundred yards distant.

They advanced closer, and continued to advance, pouring in volley after volley, till the sound of bullets over our head reminded me of a hail storm—We waited impatiently for the word of command It was at length given, "fire." One loud peal of thunder was heard from our Missouri rifles. Consternation and dismay was the result, for, thrown into confusion, the Mexicans commenced obliquing to our left.

Another volley, well aimed, caused them to *retreat* towards our wagons. Here they were met by a round from the wagon company. In the meantime Captain Reed, at the lead of eighteen men, well mounted, pushed after them basing them to the mountains. All their provisions guns, sabres, camp furniture, &c., besides one 10 pound howitzer fell into our hands. The Mexican loss was estimated at thirty or forty killed and wounded, while we had but two slightly wounded. The Mexicans left their dead on the field.

26th.—With fifteen prisoners, and a few wounded Mexicans, we resumed our march, the main army being flanked on both sides, and came on sixteen miles and encamped in a desolate place, filled with thorn bushes. Here we prepared our supper, and were about to sit down, when the report of a gun from the picket guard, caused us to extinguish the fires, and form in line as quickly as possible. Presently our lieutenant rode up and said it was a false alarm. We were ordered to break ranks and get our supper.

Again we commenced that unfortunate meal, when the report of a second gun, so loud as to be heard by everyone, again made us put the fires down. There was a tremendous clattering of arms, for all formed in line in a few seconds. At this moment Lieut. Cribbons rode up, and said that on visiting one of the outer pickets, he was requested to give the countersign by the guard, whose gun was cocked, and he accidentally let the hammer down too heavily, causing it to explode, the load passing close to the lieutenant's face. After hearing this statement, we again broke ranks, to resume our supper. I stood sentinel, to guard the wagons and a piece of artillery taken from the enemy, till 12 o'clock, then went to bed; was awakened again at 3, and stood till 6 o'clock.

Sunday, 27th.—Col. Doniphan wishing an early start, the roll was called at light, and we moved on in the same order as yesterday, with front and rear guard. We had scarcely travelled six miles, when at a distance over the river was seen a dust as if a body of horsemen were meeting us. We were told to keep cool, and obey orders. Continuing our course, we met several Mexicans bearing a white flag. Their commander coming up, presented Colonels Doniphan and Mitchell his sabre. They then drank wine and other liquors together, and we resumed our march, crossed the Rio Grande, and encamped in the town of El Paso del Norte about nightfall.

This is the noted pass between Old and New Mexico. The town contains about seven or eight thousand inhabitants, and is built along the margin of the river, several miles in length. The environs are cultivated to some extent, and the usual varieties of fruit grow here in abundance. The river is compressed in many places to a very small compass, by the high and precipitous mountains, through which it winds its way.

28th.—Established our quarters a mile from the city, where there is a large coral or enclosure, in which to keep our horses. Throughout the day a variety of fruit was brought to camp by the natives, and readily bought up by the soldiers. The wind was high, and we were nearly blinded by clouds of dust, which being mixed with isinglass is very hurtful to the eyes.

29th.—Today Col. Doniphan, while searching the town, found two pieces of cannon, and after breaking several locks, a good deal of ammunition was discovered. We all paraded and were carried through the regular drill.

January 1st, 1847.—The last two days being quite cold, with high winds, we kept in camp. After the usual parade today. Lieutenant Todd went to town about 10 o'clock in company with several of our men, but they returned in a short time at full speed, hallooing with all their might for us to get our horses quickly, and saddle up, for the Mexicans were coming on us. In a little while we were ready and marched over the river to join the other regiment, and prepared for battle.

When we arrived at the ground, we were formed by Col. Doniphan, who dispatched Col. Mitchell with twelve men to reconnoitre the enemy, who were reported to be in sight. In the course of an hour, they returned and said it was a false alarm. We were marched to the public square, and informed by our captain that arrangements were made to keep us in town, and that our camp equipage must be sent for. One out of each mess was directed to go with the wagons for that purpose. We were well supplied with fuel at night, and our quarters were quite comfortable.

2nd.—Nothing of importance transpired today. The roll was called, and we paraded twice, morning and evening.

Sunday 3rd.—The usual duties being over and a high wind prevailing, we did not go to church. Hearing that a sick horse was in the coral I went over to see, and found it was my mare. I brought her out to have her bled and physicked. I went to get assistance, and when I returned with a friend I found she had escaped; searched the town three hours without finding her.

4th.—Renewed my efforts to recover my lost horse; walked till 3 o'clock, when I found her in the centre of a lot about two miles from town—dead. I hastened to Col. Mitchell and told him I was on foot, as my mare had lost breath and was laid up to dry. He advised me to look about and ascertain if I could suit myself. If I succeeded I was to call on him again in the morning.

5th.—Our orderly sergeant in reading over the names of those to be placed on mounted guard, cried out mine. Accordingly, I with three others marched down to the public square, where we paraded, and dinner, or rather supper, being over, we were placed as sentinels till three o'clock in the morning. I then went to the guard fire, spread down my blanket and slept till daylight.

6th.—Today we are allowed two-third rations of coarse Taos flour, some coffee without sugar, and poor mutton. We sometimes got a few peaches from the inhabitants in exchange for tobacco, buttons, &c.

7th.—Finding our flour nearly gone I went out and bought a baked pumpkin to mix with it; saw much fruit exhibited for sale, but had no money to buy any. Our scouting party which had heed sent out a few days ago, returned this evening, bringing three prisoners, a priest among them. They were captured twelve miles down, on their way to Chihuahua, with papers containing information of our movements to the Mexican army in that quarter. They were placed under strict surveillance.

Sunday, 10th.—I went to church with a number of others, and witnessed ail the ceremonies, and manoeuvres of this singular people. The church is large, and the handsomest and best built house in the place. I saw the representation of Christ in the sepulchre, with various other images in and near the alter. On our return, we found multitudes in the open street, playing cards—-sorry to say, some were American soldiers.

13th.—Our time begins to hang heavily. The ordinary duties of the day are soon accomplished, and no novelty to amuse or excite, the soldiers become restless, and are ready for any excess. Our living consists of poor mutton, the miserable Taos flour, and a little coffee. Some complain, and others "hook" what they can to improve their fare.

14th.—I was taken last night with a violent headache and a pain in the bowels. My diarrhoea having become much worse, I got up and went to the surgeon, who gave me 15 grs. calomel, 10 *do.* jalap, 5 *do.* rhubarb, and 2 *do.* tarter, all mixed up together in a dose. I took this monstrous compound, and sat by the guard-fire till morning; I then laid on my blanket, and slept till 3 o'clock in the evening. Needing some refreshment, I tried my mess, but they had nothing I could relish, and I then went to Sergeant Edwards, who gave me a lump of sugar to sweeten my coffee.

I tried in vain to borrow a *picayune* to purchase some molasses. At length I applied to a mess-mate, who had come to me a few days after my horse had died, bringing a mule, and saying if I would consent to let him draw the rations of my horse, I should have the use of this mule. Yesterday I understood he had sent his mule away to graze, and was selling my corn. When I presented my petition, he turned his back as a refusal, and went down among the gamblers, and lost every cent.

15th.—Feeling disordered and ill, I applied early to our surgeon, who gave me a small lump of sugar, charging me to take particular care of the article, as it was only intended for the sick. He felt my pulse, and made me swallow a large dose of salts and tarter; I then went to my blanket.

16th.—I awoke this morning with a high fever and headache. The surgeon gave me a large pill, and I was placed in the hospital, under the particular care of a doctor, whose name I could not learn, but who said he was from Philadelphia, and could out-practice any man in the regiment. Wishing some coffee, he very politely took a pinch of sugar between his thumb and finger, to sweeten it for me, talking the while of "his superior skill," &c.

17th.—Still in the hospital, but feeling better, I applied to the quarter master, who gave me four pints of American flour; I baked a small cake to eat with my coffee. At night I spread my blanket in the tent, and slept with my mess.

18th.—At the sound of the reveille I arose and strolled over the grave yard, where the remains of young Leland were interred yesterday. This young man died of the fever prevailing among the troops, and his grave is close to the wall, fronting an old church in ruins. Piles of bones lay around; in the centre of some hills were erected wooden crosses.

21st.—Since Tuesday last I have been ill in the hospital, with a high fever and headache; bed hard and uncomfortable, consequently little sleep or rest. The doctor, in his round, asked me why I was not out at the roll-call this morning, as my name was erased, by his direction, from the sick list. He said there was nothing the matter with me, and he would give me no more medicine. He charged me with being homesick, &c., &c., with many other *tender* and *endearing* epithets. Weak and quite unwell, I left the hospital, and found my way to Colonel Doniphan's quarters; consulted Dr. Morton, who, with expressions of sympathy, gave me the necessary restoratives. I had symptoms of jaundice, with very sore eyes.

26th.—I was somewhat recovered from my illness, through the humane treatment of Dr. Morton, but I still suffered considerably from my eyes. I felt much regret that I was prevented from joining Captain Hudson, who took our company on a scout, and will be gone several days. I begin to feel weary of our detention here, occasioned by the non-arrival of Capt. Weightman with the artillery from Santa Fe. Colonel Doniphan is hourly expecting this reinforcement.

27th.—Last evening a fellow was caught by our outer picket guard, who could give no satisfactory account of himself, and told so many contradictory tales, that our colonel sent him to the guard-house. At ten o'clock our company returned from the scouting expedition; they went down to the fort, twenty-five miles off, and found it was deserted. They think it very likely we shall have no fighting to do at Chihuahua.

29th.—While on guard today over the prisoners taken at the battle of Bracito, I thought I would write in my *journal*; I searched my belt for it in vain. It was gone!—taken out probably by some mischievous soldier in the tent. In this book I had faithfully kept an account of everything *interesting to myself* at least, since the day I left Carroll County, Missouri. Having another blank book I commenced writing again, but felt provoked at my loss.

30th.—This morning, being relieved from the duty of sentinel, I went immediately to Captain Hudson and stated the loss of my *jour-*

nal. He asked me a number of questions in relation to it, and appeared pleased at so unusual an undertaking in a private. He went forward and told the soldiers that Maryland's book must be restored or every man in his command should be searched.

31st.—The impatience of our boys for the arrival of the artillery has induced several to go out to meet it. This evening some of them returned, and said it was not more than thirty miles off. Today my book was found on the floor of the tent. The robber was no doubt alarmed by the captain's order, and dropped it in the most convenient place.

February 1st.—We paraded early, and about 12 o'clock several rounds from our artillery-men, just across the Rio Grande, announced the arrival of Capt. Weightman from Santa Fe, with four six pounders and two twelve pound howitzers. They marched in town in right order; our men firing the salute from our piece of captured cannon just as they reached the public square. This company is an important acquisition to our small force.

3rd.—Early orders were received that Lieutenant Col. Mitchell, at the head of the Chihuahua Rangers, would move down to the fort today. Everything being in readiness we came on in double file, and arrived at sunset at a pretty little village. Our provision wagons being delayed on the road, everything like food in this small place was had in requisition by the orders of the Colonel, and we made our supper on pies, cheese, bread, &c.

4th.—This morning we were told to saddle up and hasten forward to overtake the traders, who had disobeyed orders in preceding us, we were ordered to bring them back. In obedience to the orders we started and travelled thirteen miles. On the way we saw several Mexicans, who endeavoured to elude our observation. Our first and second lieutenants wishing to know who they were, and on what errand bent, gave chase. After a run of two miles at full speed, they were overtaken and searched. One was the *alcade* from the town where we staid last night. We halted late in the evening on the road, where we met a Mexican fully armed, gun, sabre, &c. He was also stopped and minutely examined, but no papers being found on his person, he was suffered to pass.

5th.—Marched on several miles, overtook and encamped with the traders, who had formed their wagons in a pen or coral, tried to refresh ourselves on a supper of black bread, poor beef, and sassafras tea, cooked over a fire of thorn bushes. The traders sell the bark of the sassafras at $1 per pound. A small cup of the decoction cost 25 cents tonight.

6th.—The ground was so uneven we did not erect our tents, but spread our blankets and went to bed; the cold prevented anything like refreshing sleep. We arrived late at our former encampment, and found Colonel Mitchell had returned from El Paso, whither he had gone to see Col. Doniphan. He brought news which was currently reported there, *viz.* that Gen. Taylor had been overpowered at San Louis Potosi by the Mexicans, and was imprisoned, with 4000 regulars. Of course this was a Mexican story, told no doubt for effect—and it had its effect upon our boys, for it made us feel as if we could fight like lions against the treacherous foe. We waited at this place for Col. Doniphan, who was making every preparation for our dangerous trip. I made for my own use today a pair of wooden spurs.

7th.—This morning after roll call and breakfast, we fed our horses and mules, and tried to rest and amuse ourselves. At supper I made some pancakes, without milk or eggs; unfortunately I put rather too much salt in my batter. Fifteen men were sent down the river on a scouting expedition tonight. My name was called to be guards so I gathered up my blanket, and went into the line with the rest. I was placed in the first relief, near the river. I walked two hours, then went to bed at 12 o'clock, by the guard-fire; I was awakened by the corporal at three, and stood till morning.

8th.—Prepared my clothes by washing and mending, for our departure. Boiled some beans and beef for my mess. The weather was very disagreeable, and we all felt weary of our delay.

9th.—While busily engaged fixing up today. Colonel Doniphan came on with the artillery, and encamped near us. All is now bustle and excitement, as it is said we will start in the morning.

10th.—Col. Doniphan has concluded to stay here today with the army, as it is very cold and cloudy. Our boys are making desperate efforts to amuse themselves. Among other things, our sutler is here, with his establishment, and whiskey is selling at 75 cents per pint With some honourable exceptions, the scenes among officers and men may be much "better imagined than described."

11th.—The whole of Colonel Doniphan's regiment, including the Chihuahua Rangers, started this morning for the South to join General Wool. We marched in right order twelve miles, and encamped on the bank of the river.

12th.—The wagons not coming in last night, some uneasiness was expressed by our commander, when, with fifteen others, I returned to where we encamped the night before, and found the train just about to move on. We passed a caravan, who told us they had lost the last night 250 mules and 50 yoke of oxen, driven off by the Indians. We came to our camp and found cooking to be the order of the day. We are about entering another *jornada*, and provisions for four days must be packed.

13th.—Detained here to have all in complete readiness. The Indians were at their thievish work again. Last night they drove off some cattle and mules belonging to the traders. The skill and daring evinced by these bands of savages, exceed belief. They follow the army, and are always prowling around our camp at night.

Sunday, 14th.— Although on mounted guard nearly all night, I made all the haste I could to eat an early breakfast and saddle up. I was among the first in the ranks. Here we were told that the burial of two soldiers, who expired last night, would only detain us a few minutes longer. The mournful ceremony ended, we started at 8 o'clock; came on the *jornada* five miles, and halted to feed our horses and mules. I was in the rear guard behind the prisoners all day; travelled a long and wearisome journey through the sand, until 8 o'clock at night. I ate a small piece of bread and meat, and spread my blanket at the guard-fire, where I slept till four. I was awakened by the officer of the watch, and stood till six. I was at last relieved by the sound of the tattoo.

15th.—Twelve miles further on we stopped to eat breakfast, which was a cold cut. We again moved on, and came twenty miles through this *jornada*, and encamped late in the night. No water was as yet to be seen. Our sergeant measured to each man a half pint. One man sold his half pint for 50 cents.

16th.—We made an early start, and after marching fifteen miles, came to some puddles of dirty water. Our horses and mules rushed in and drank all they could get. Ascending the hill before us, a spring was discovered, but the water was muddy and brackish. At night had a slight shower of rain, with lightning and thunder.

17th.—On awaking, the first thing I heard, was that a man in our company was dead. The poor fellow had left a wife and family in Missouri to serve his country. He was taken sick at El Paso, with the measles, and had come thus far to die. We followed his remains to the grave, where our captain stood forth and made an impressive speech. He stated that "this was the third time he had been called, on occasions like the present, to perform the mournful duty to men in his command, and that it was wisdom for each and all to prepare for the worst," &c. The usual rounds were fired, and we covered poor Tolly over with soap-weed, and filled up the grave. After trampling the dirt and levelling the ground, we marched off in right order to this spot, where we shall rest today.

18th.—Loaned my mule to a soldier who had lost his horse, to enable him to go in search. I was rewarded for this favour, by being compelled to stay behind my company several hours, till he returned with his horse. We pursued our journey two miles, and overtook the command at a Hot Spring, which was discovered on the top of a small eminence. It boiled up very curiously in the centre, covering the surface with bubbles. The temperature about 100 degrees.

The water is scarcely fit to drink, having a very disagreeable taste, nevertheless, the men filled their canteens, saying they would drink it when it got cold enough. The country still presents a barren appearance, the soil sterile; the surface rocky and mountainous. We marched fourteen miles, and about sunset, encamped close to a small stream, which supplied a few poor villages with water. The people busied themselves in preparing for us, what they could, *viz.* a little musket brush to cook with, and corn for our cattle. In crossing this *jornada*, the teamsters were obliged to throw away 5000 pounds of flour, and leave several wagons behind—the mules being unable to proceed.

19th.—After a journey of such a length over uneven ground, the fatigue of the army induced our Commander to remain in camp to-day. About two o'clock the wind began to rise, and increased in violence till the tents were levelled to the ground. We tried to cook by digging pits in which to place the fire. The sand blowing in clouds, covered our food; making it gritty and unpleasant to eat. As night came on, a heavy storm of wind stripped our wagons of their covers. Quite unsheltered, we had to do the best we could, and that was had enough. We laid down, as we had often done before, on our blankets. We slept uncomfortably on hillocks and tufts of grass.

20th.—The wind having abated, we were all in line at an early hour—came nine miles through this ranch, to the mouth of another *jornada*. Here the same scene of desolation is presented. No cultivation to be seen anywhere, nor scarcely any natural vegetable production except the thorn and *muskeet* brush. The days are warm, and the nights very cold, in this region.

21st.—Marched ten miles out to the Hot Springs, which are situated in a ranch, and encamped. The army will here halt a day or two. The same arrangements are to be made as before. While cooking my meat and bread, I was informed by the orderly, that with eighteen others, I was appointed to go before the command several miles. Hastily dispatching the meal, we mounted and rode out a long distance, where we had to stand all night. We made a small fire of brush weed on the road side.

22nd.—I was relieved from duty early this morning by the next detail. Feeling much disordered from loss of rest and fatigue, I was greatly obliged to a messmate who very thoughtfully brought me some water and a piece of bread for my breakfast. The army appearing, we went into line by sections of four, and marched seventeen miles, where we encamped at a place where the men had water; but none could be spared to the poor horses and mules. After eating some bread, we laid down on the ground and went to sleep.

23rd.—Without waiting for refreshments of any kind, we came on today eight miles to a pond, where we watered our horses and mules—we stopped for the poor animals to graze awhile, and then proceeded three miles, when we halted for the night at a stream of water. Several antelopes were killed today. After the tents were fixed up, we boiled some of the flesh, which made fine eating; the repast was seasoned with a good appetite, a fast of nearly forty-eight hours, had made us hungry enough.

24th.—In conversation with my captain, I expressed a wish to go up a neighbouring mountain, as I understood a large lagoon could be seen from its summit. He told me to go and make all the observations I could. Having no time to lose, I commenced its ascent, by climbing over large rocks, in which were formed several immense caves; some of them I thought were well fitted to be the resort of robbers. At length I found myself on the top, and sat down to write. At the distance of three miles a lake of considerable extent is seen, reposing in the bosom of a prairie, bounded by the horizon. To the left a continuous range of mountains loom up, whose bare and rugged tops present to the mind the idea of coldness and desolation. The whole face of the country is destitute of wood and *verdure*, except a species of brush or thorn bushes.

Looking towards our camp, I beheld a long line of wagons stretching along the road as far as the sight could reach. They were all in motion, and the sight made me hasten down the mountain at a brisk pace. It was our army preparing for a start, and I did not wish to be left "solitary and alone," in that rocky region. In a few minutes we took up the line of march; came twelve miles, and encamped at sunset. We saw Mexican spies at a distance. The picket guard came in and reported that 10,000 Mexicans were at a lake some miles off, ready to give us battle.

25th.—The sound of the reveille started every man to his post by light. We moved on eight miles to the lake, and watered our horses and mules. We saw nothing of the Mexicans. The country begins to improve as we leave the *jornada*, especially on the margin of these lakes or ponds, the water of which is brackish. Here prairie grass grows with some luxuriance. Kindling a fire, the soldiers commenced baking bread, made from the wretched native flour, now our only fare. A high wind prevailing, sparks were carried out, which set the dry brush and weeds in a flame. The Chihuahua Rangers had orders to subdue the fire, and we commenced threshing it out with our blankets, but the wind increasing, we found it useless labour. The flames continued to increase in spite of us. The whole command was put in action with their horses, beating a track, to stop the progress of the fire.

Unfortunately for us, the fire caught the grass on the other side of the track, and the wind blowing tremendously, the fire was carried in almost every direction. We then encamped on the burnt ground, off of which the grass had been burnt, and picketing our horses on the left of the road in the prairie, we laid down to rest. In a few hours we were awakened to bring our horses in, for the whole prairie was on fire. Coming out of my tent, a sight appeared of such magnificence as had never before met my eyes. It was an opposite mountain on fire, and the whole prairie, as far as the eye could reach, in flames. A strange glare tinged the clouds, and all surrounding objects, and presented a scene which was fearfully grand. It consumed nearly all the grass in the country fifteen miles towards Chihuahua.

26th.—We continued winding through the mountain passes and plains sixteen miles. Our advance found a coral today, in which were fifty sheep and fifteen cattle, driven in from the surrounding neighbourhood. They were immediately butchered for the command, the soldiers being nearly exhausted for want of food. This was a dreadful day for our march. The wind was so high that we could scarcely see a hundred yards ahead.

27th.—The artillery and wagons were kept in front all day, the whole army being formed in two lines in the rear. We marched in right order eight miles, and encamped on the margin of a lake. Here we shall halt till tomorrow. Scouts were sent out in every direction. I was busily engaged writing for our boys, who believe themselves to be on the eve of some engagement with the enemy. Saw several of our men come in, leading a horse; soon learned that spies being seen by our advance, Capt. Skillman of the traders' company, and Capt. Parsons of the E company from Cole County, with others, gave chase, and overtook one. The fellow, finding he was likely to become a prisoner, leaped off, and fled up the mountain, leaving his horse and all his rigging behind. He was elegantly mounted. Col. Mitchell has just informed us that a battle will be fought tomorrow.

BATTLE OF SACRAMENTO.

Sunday, 28th.—At sunrise this morning, we took up our line of march, having learned from our spies that the enemy in great numbers, had fortified the pass of the River Sacramento, about fifteen miles off. Our trains consisting of 315 traders' wagons, and our commissary and company wagons, in all about 400, were formed into four columns, so as to shorten our lines. The whole command marched In right order between the columns, thus concealing our force from the enemy. When we arrived within three miles of their entrenchments, Col. Doniphan made a reconnoisance of their position, and examined the arrangements of their forces. This was easily done, as our road led through an open prairie valley between the high mountains.

The pass of the Sacramento is formed by a point of the mountains on our right, their left extending into the valley, so as to narrow the valley about one and a half miles. On our left was a deep, dry channel of a creek, and between these points, the plain rises abruptly about fifty or sixty feet. The road passes down the centre of the valley, and in the distance we had a full view of the Mexican army. On the point of the mountains, they had a battery of four guns, so elevated as to sweep the plain. On the left, there was another battery commanding the road, with six pounders and rampart pieces, mounted on carriages. Their cavalry was drawn up in front of their redoubts, in the interval of four deep.

When we had arrived near their entrenchments, our columns suddenly diverged to the right, so as to gain the elevation, which the enemy endeavoured to prevent by moving forward with four pieces of cannon and 1000 cavalry. But our movements were so rapid, that we not only gained the eminence, but were formed in order for their reception. Our company (Capt. Hudson's) now dismounted, and every eighth man was detailed, to hold horses and mules. It fell to my lot to hold eight mules. The action now commenced by a brisk fire from our cannons, doing considerable execution at the distance of twelve hundred yards, killing fifteen of the enemy, and disabling one of their guns.

Our fire was briskly returned from fourteen pieces of artillery, sending ragged balls, and heavy copper ore. But being badly aimed they stuck in the ground about forty or fifty yards before us, and rebounding passed over our heads without harm, except slightly wounding two men, and killing several horses and mules in the rear. Our guns were so well aimed as to compel the enemy to fall behind the breastworks. We resumed our march in our former order, diverging as much as possible to the right, to avoid a heavy battery, and their strongest redoubts, which were on our left, near the common road.

After marching as far as we thought it prudent, without coming in range of their heavy battery, Capt. Weightman of the artillery, was ordered to charge it with two 12 lb. howitzers, to be supported by the cavalry, under Captains Reid, Parsons and Hudson. We then remounted and charged the battery from right to left, with a brisk and deadly fire from our rifles. We then advanced to the very brink of their redoubts, and drove them out with our sabres.

The enemy now fell back on their centre battery, where they made a desperate rally, and gave us a shower of balls and copper ore, which whizzed over our heads without doing us any injury except wounding several men and killing a few mules and horses. Major Clarke was ordered to commence a heavy fire upon this battery which being well directed, together with the rapid advance of our columns, put them to flight over the mountains in utter confusion, leaving all their cannons, and the ground strewed with their dead and wounded.

Thus ended the battle of Sacramento, which commenced about three o'clock, and ended about sunset The enemy numbered 4220 rank and file, and lost 300 killed 600 wounded, besides forty prisoners The American force consisted of 924 effective men, 1 killed, 11 wounded. Our success is to be attributed entirely to the superior skill of our commander. Had he not taken advantage of position, in keeping out of range of redoubts and batteries we should all have shared a common fate, as the back piratical flag was captured, together with a wagon load of that formidable weapon, the lariat, which was intended to tie us all to our saddles in case of a defeat.

The Mexicans lost ten pieces of artillery, varying from five to ten lbs. and seven one lb. culverines One of the cannon is very valuable, being composed of silver and brass melted together They also lost all their baggage, ammunition, &c., and provisions enough to last us three months were found in their wagons, together with $4000 in specie. It was gratifying to see the soldiers shaking hands with their officers after the engagement, and tendering their congratulations to their commander for his skill and bravery displayed on this memorable occasion.

The surgeons are now busily engaged in administering relief to the wounded Mexicans, and it is a sight to see the pile of legs and arms that have been amputated. The cries and groans of the poor fellows, are distressing in the extreme. It is a fact worthy of note, that the atmosphere here in this mountainous region is so perfectly pure and clear that a cannon shot can be seen coming, When it is a considerable distance off, by leaving a blue streak in the air. Many a soldier saved his life in the battle by dodging the balls as they came forward. When a flash would be seen from the enemy's battery, you could hear the soldiers cry out—"watch the ball boys!—here comes a ball boys," and they invariably avoided them, or the slaughter must have been very great.

I saw a ball coming in the direction where I was, when immediately falling off my mule, it passed just over my saddle without injury. Our rapid movements seemed to astonish the enemy. Our four pieces of flying artillery, discharging five times in a minute, volleys of grape and canister, with chain shots, would rake the enemy's redoubts and cut roads through their lines, while our 12lb. howitzers throwing a constant shower of bombs into the middle of their entrenchments, and the unerring aim of our Mississippi rifles, acting in concert, cast terror and dismay among the cowardly and unprincipled foe.

Our men acted nobly, and in the hand to hand fight in the redoubts they fought to desperation. Lieutenant Sprawl, our 2nd lieutenant, a man over six feet high, with bared arms, and without his hat, his long hair, and beard streaming in the wind, with sword in hand, was charging the enemy at every point, when a ball struck his splendid charger, and he fell. But seizing his carbine he kept up with us on foot.

Another of our men, being unhorsed, and fighting near me, was attacked by a Mexican, who was about to lance him, and the poor fellow's gun being discharged, he picked up a rock, and throwing it, struck his enemy on the head, which felled him to the earth, when he knocked his brains out with the butt of his gun. These were but common occurrences in that hard contested fight, where we had to contend with nearly five to one.

March 1st.—After spending a comfortable night, feasting on the good things of our enemy, and making our prisoners bury the dead, we started with the remains of Major Owings, and after marching four miles encamped. My mule having received a wound in the loins yesterday, cannot be found this morning, so I borrowed one of the commissary.

2nd.—Placed on mounted guard to precede the army, whose entrance in the city will take place today. Came ten miles; saw the spire of the cathedral towering in the distance with peculiar feelings of delight. A merrier group could scarcely be pictured than our worthy Colonel Mitchell and his escort. We entered the beautiful city of Chihuahua about 12 o'clock, and proceeded immediately to the *plaza* or public square. The inhabitants are polite, and manifest, in various ways, the utmost complaisance and regard to our soldiery. Of course we see the fairest specimens of Mexican character here, and afford us evidences of superior intelligence, comfort, and industry.

While the soldiers were scattered in various directions, seeking refreshments, I took a walk alone, and seated myself in a quiet nook, fronting the cathedral. It is an imposing structure of white marble. It was about fifty years in building—the production of a gold mine—and cost *three millions of dollars.* I felt too much fatigued to write a long description of even a beautiful church, although, had it been otherwise, such employment would have been pleasant to me. The tones of the bell are grand. It strikes the hour, and can be heard at a great distance.

At sundown Col. Doniphan arrived in town with the rest of the command, all in fine order. The band was playing Washington's March; just as we reached the public square, the tune was changed to Yankee Doodle, when there was a general huzza. We then marched through the town, and took up our quarters on the outskirts. I was placed on picket guard, and had to be up all night—first to watch the prisoners, and then to walk my post three hours.

3rd.—All is now tranquil. The funeral of Major Owings took place today. Everything was conducted with the utmost decency and order.

4th.—This morning I sallied forth for a ramble. I went through the thickest parts of the city, which I should judge, contained about 40,000 inhabitants. The streets cross at right angles, and the houses are mostly built of the usual sun-dried brick, in Mexican style, with flat roofs, and close barred windows, as if intended for defence against street assaults, or rival factions. I was, afterwards, introduced to some *senoras*, and drank some coffee with them—they using the *ardiente* instead of cream in theirs.

5th.—Passing near the public square, I encountered Col. Mitchell, with several officers on horseback, before a handsome building. The colonel was earnestly engaged in conversation with a man who, it appeared, was an Englishman. I soon learned that our colonel wished to search the building, but the English gentleman said he should not. I was called on, with several others, who were standing near, to form ranks, and go at once and arm ourselves. We ran to our quarters, and soon returned well equipped. I had not been in the line more than a minute, when I saw my entire company, the Chihuahua Rangers, come up. I, of course, left my position, and with them paraded before the house.

The Englishman being still very stubborn, and refusing to give up the keys, the colonel ordered two pieces of artillery to be brought down immediately, and placed before the door. Turning to look for the man, I found he had escaped to the top of a house, not far off, where he stationed himself to watch our movements. He no sooner espied the cannon, than he ran down in great haste, begging for a few minutes to open the door, saying "somebody might be killed," &c. We then entered peaceably. Magoffin, the trader, whom the authorities of the city had condemned to death as a traitor, cannot be found. On inquiry, we learned that he had been sent to Durango. But several are of opinion that he has been killed.

6th.—I went to the secretary's office and wrote letters to my sisters in Maryland.

10th—For several days past we have been relieved from all extra duty, only answering the roll-call night and morning. I have been busily engaged today writing letters for different persons.

17th.—During the past week I have had no time to write in my *journal.* I have been busy waiting letters for others, and assisting in writing out requisitions, &c. I received tonight the first number of the *Anglo Saxon*, a paper printed by our boys, and the first American newspaper ever published in Chihuahua. On Wednesday the 16th, the express started from here for the United States. Many weary months have passed, and we have heard no tidings from home and friends. Truly a soldier's lot is a hard one.

19th.—I had a chill last night, which ended in a fever. I felt thankful that I was favoured with every attention from Lieut. Sprawl, who is as kind and generous as he s brave. A few hours sleep recovered me in some degree from the stupidity in which the fever left me, and I arose from the stone floor refreshed. I went to church, which was opened for Mass, but soon returned with a headache, longing for the simple and sweet worship of my own church at home. An express, consisting of twelve men, was sent on to General Taylor today.

20th.—I took a stroll through the town; went down to the American Hotel to learn what news was stirring. Nothing is heard from the South.

23rd.—We have at this time all that is necessary for our comfort, and nothing to do but attend to our slight duties, and take care of our mules and horses. A strict guard is kept. The captured cannon is in charge of the non-commissioned officers, and our company has to practice target shooting. Being number four, I have to touch off the guns. The concussion jars my head so much that I have to place a quid of tobacco in *each* cheek to prevent it from injuring my teeth which are very sore The companies are all well disciplined, and with our twenty-five pieces of artillery, Colonel Doniphan says he would defy 10,000 Mexicans.

When not on duty, our men resort , to every kind of mischief by way of amusement Two pieces of artillery, found at this place, were, by them on yesterday, dismounted and blown up. They were filled with powder and plugged, and the muzzles being buried in the earth several feet, a slow match was applied. The reports were terrific. They have also burnt all the powder A train, nearly one-fourth of a mile in length, was made and set off, and which ignited several barrels at its termination. The poor affrighted Mexicans meanwhile ran off, crying "*no wano, no wano*," (very bad, very bad.)

Another species of fun, consists in collecting all the dogs that can be found during the day, and carefully shutting them in a room; at night each dog is brought out, and a large bundle of fireworks fastened to his tail. He is then let loose, amid the general halloo; and being enveloped in sparks, accompanied with the noise of small firearms, wherever he runs in the crowded streets, the Mexican fly before him with the utmost consternation.

Sunday, April 4th.—This was the appointed morning for us to leave Chihuahua for the south. But on account of a bullfight, our trip is postponed. As soon as church was over, the soldiers hastened to see this great sight. As I was conscientious in regard to the violation of the Sabbath, I, of course, staid behind; I was, however, informed by the men on their return, that five bulls were let loose, but none were killed. If they cannot strike the animal in some vital part, they are obliged to let him live. The blows were badly dealt, and the bull escaped. This is a strange mixture of Christianity with the barbarities of heathenism.

Card playing, cock fighting, bull baiting, and dancing, are the chief amusements of these people, and they are always accompanied with excessive drinking, not unfrequently with quarrelling and fighting, in which the belligerents are bruised, their limbs broken, and their lives sometimes destroyed. What an idea of the character of God must be entertained in the midst of such performances? He can hardly be regarded as a God of love, whose delight is in the up- right walk and chaste conversation of his people. The service of that blinded population, comports better with what we might suppose would be the worship of the devil, were such worship distinctly ordered! Alas! for the darkness in which so many of our race are enveloped!

5th.—The wagons were loaded for our long journey—but a difficulty in getting our soldiers together detained us till two o'clock, p. m. At length, everything being in readiness, we started out of town. Some of our men imagined themselves commanders in chief, assumed to give orders, and were otherwise troublesome. We succeeded in reaching a ranch, twelve miles off, and encamped.

6th.—Moved on twenty-five miles, and stopped at a ranch late in the evening. Putting our horses in a clover field, we spread our blankets on the ground and rested till morning.

7th.—After accomplishing another twenty-five miles today, we erected our tents close to the walls of a town. Here we were joined by two strangers, who said they came from a coral, 140 miles off, to inform us that a large Mexican force of about 10,000 soldiers were on their way to retake Chihuahua. They also stated that Generals Taylor and Wool had gone far to the south, in the direction of the city of Mexico. These men being native Americans induced our colonel to listen to their story, which if true, would have placed us in a bad situation With one half of our command left behind at Chihuahua, we could be easily cut off from this point.

8th.—This morning we had orders to start back to Chihuahua. After marching twenty-five miles reached the second ranch, and encamped.

9th.—Our sergeant woke us all at two o clock to get our breakfast, and make an early start. We travelled briskly thirty-six miles, and arrived at Chihuahua about four o'clock. Here we are again in the city, at our old quarters.

14th.—I have been employed in writing for our surgeon and others, for several days past. Yesterday we heard that Vera Cruz was taken by Gen. Scott. Twenty-eight rounds were fired by our artillery-men.

15th.—I witnessed today the mode of punishment among the Mexicans, and felt disgusted at the sight. Offenders are tied to a tree and severely lashed for different offences. I saw several whipped today for horse stealing. At night it commenced raining. The first rain since we have been in the city. I was too sick to perform the duty of sentinel.

16th.—The morning air being clear and cool I took a walk to relieve the excessive languor I feel. I have little or no appetite, and my spirits are very much depressed. I went to the American hotel, where a great many questions were asked me. While there I read an advertisement of a grand ball to be given on Sunday, 18th, enhance $2. It is really distressing to contemplate the desecration of the Sabbath in this country. Oh! how I long to be once more in a truly Christian land, and among congenial spirits.

Sunday, 18th.—Various exhibitions encountered at every step throughout the city today. Sunday as it is, gambling is the most prominent. At night the greater part of our men went to the ball.

19th.—Drew off some writing for our doctor; afterwards, with a messmate, took a bath in the river—still quite sick, and nothing to eat, but poor beef, with bread and coffee. This stone floor is particularly hard to rest on.

24th.—I went with a Mexican to see the *prison*. He was very polite and accommodating; he took me through the cells, and showed me the blocks, and chains, handcuffs, lariats, &c., that had been prepared to keep all the prisoners safely, which they expected to have taken in the battle. They were to have been kept here until they could be marched on foot to the city of Mexico. But they counted their game a little the soon! The prison is the darkest and most gloomy place I ever saw.

Sunday morning, 25th.—Just as the church bells began to ring, our men geared up their mules, and at 11 o'clock, two companies started out of town with the artillery, and arrived about three o'clock at the first ranch.

26th.—An early start took us to the second ranch twenty-five miles. Tonight our second battalion came up.

27th.—After marching thirty-six miles today we came to a town called Santa Cruz, where we encamped.

28th.—We lay by here, and wait for the rest of the army, which will start from Chihuahua today.

29th.—At daybreak we set out, and after marching twenty-one miles, came to Sousilla, a town situated on the River Couchas, which is, at that place, a considerable stream. I went with one or two hundred others, and took a refreshing bath. At night I cooked a supper of coarse bread, beef and coffee, with the materials of a coral, which we tore down.

30th.—Still travelling on the Rio Couchas. Passed a town called Los Cruezas, and at the end of twenty-eight miles encamped at the town of San Rosalia. Col. Doniphan's first battalion came up tonight.

May 1st.—At the sound of the reveille all went in line, and after roll-call our captain told us to get our arms in good order for inspection at nine o'clock. Every man was soon busy firing off loaded guns, cleaning out, &c. Tonight I went into town and brought a welcome repast for my mess, *viz.* pork-steak and nice bread.

2nd.—Our captain, after calling the roll, told us that the reveille had sounded thus early for a company to go in advance. Came out a few miles and stopped to inspect a fort the Mexicans had erected to keep Gen. Wool from marching to Chihuahua. It is nicely finished off, with port holes for their batteries, &c. The building covers nearly an acre of ground; but everything is silent, the place being entirely deserted. A fatiguing march of twenty-seven miles brought us to a ranch called Remado, where we passed the night.

3rd.—The country is still barren between these *ranchos*, which are always found in fertile valleys, mostly inhabited. Some *muskeet* brush was all we could find on our road today; no verdant carpet of grass to relieve the eye from the strong glare of the rays of the sun pouring on the sandy plains as we passed along. A late hour brought us to a large town called Huadaquiila, on the Rio Florida. We travelled thirty miles today.

4th.—At ten we left—came out six miles and encamped. On our way we saw several monuments erected to various saints. A pile of rocks marks the grave of one great personage. In the centre of the pile is erected a cross, adorned with artificial flowers. The country around this town is cultivated; provisions are cheap and plenty. All the soldiers are now engaged in packing provisions and water; the latter precious article, it is said, will not be found again till sixty-five miles are passed over. At four, p. m., we came on and travelled twenty-five miles in this *jornada*, and laid ourselves down to sleep in the sand, after taking a cut of meat and bread at nearly 12 o'clock.

5th.—By the time it was light our orderly came around to rouse us to roll-call. Some poor fellows, half asleep, staggered off into ranks. We started and marched forty miles through a thick dust, when we came to a pond of brackish water, which is sometimes found in these deserts. Here we halted for the night. The water was quickly drank by our famishing boys, notwithstanding it was a disagreeable mixture of salt and sulphur.

6th.—The fatigue and sufferings of yesterday were not allayed by a report in camp that several thousand Mexicans were lying in wait a few miles ahead, in order to cut off our artillery. We marched on ten miles and stopped on the banks of the Rio Cerro Gordo, where we have tolerably good water.

7th.—I arose from the guard-fire, where I had been stretched the last three hours dull and sleepy, having been on duty all the former part of the night; I went to my mess, whom I found eating breakfast. As soon as we got through, our command started and travelled thirty miles. Here we stopped at a ranch, near which are several springs bursting from a bank, the water of which is very clear, but very warm, and of a most disagreeable taste. A few hundred yards from the camp we saw a large deserted fort, also a coral, which our boys tore down to cook with. The face of the country has nothing to recommend it, but a vast variety of cactus, beautifully in bloom all over the sandy plains. Covered with dust, I found a bath in the hot springs very refreshing tonight.

Sunday, 9th.—Pursued our way uninterruptedly the past two days and travelled forty miles. At night we encamped at a town called Mapemilla. At our approach the inhabitants tied to the mountains. It was a fine night, and their fires in the distance, dotting the mountain side, had a singular and romantic effect. News met us here that Gen. Scott had whipped Santa Anna, which caused Col. Doniphan to fire a salute of twenty-nine rounds.

20th.—At 3 o'clock this morning the reveille sounded. A little coarse bread, and coffee without sugar, constituted breakfast, on which we travelled thirty miles. We halted late at night, at a ranch called San Sebastian, on the Rio Mosas, a stream sufficiently large for swimming. It was soon covered with our soldiers enjoying this rare luxury.

11th.—At an early hour we had to bury two of our men, who died yesterday. They were found last night, (after our fatiguing march of thirty miles,) dead in the wagons. They were buried in a warlike manner. We crossed the river two miles below the town, and pursued our route thirty miles to another village, called San Lorenzo. Here we encamped, but suffered much inconvenience from want of water, having to use it very sparingly. Tonight another grave was opened for another of our men.

12th.—As usual, our whole command was put in motion at three o'clock, and after marching seven miles through a thick dust, had orders to halt and turn back, for we had left the right road behind. Our army turned about and travelled several miles until we got right. At the end of eighteen miles we encamped on the Rio Mosas. Here, unable to join the swimmers, from a violent attack of earache, accompanied with a most painful sore mouth, which latter I have suffered with since leaving Chihuahua, I went to a Dutch surgeon for advice. He looked in my mouth a few seconds, and with an air of confidence declared that *nothing ailed me*. I determined thereafter to bear my pains like a hero, and almost vowed that I would never pester a Dutchman either for his sympathy or his prescriptions.

13th.—This morning we started early, and after travelling thirty miles, reached a ranch. The first objects that I met our eyes, were six Indians lying dead. They had been killed by our advance guard of about thirty rank and file, under Captain Reid. The guard was unexpectedly attacked by a body of Indians, which they repulsed, after killing thirteen of their number, with their chief. He must have been a desperate warrior, for even after he was shot down, and to the last moment of his life, he tried to use his bow and arrows.

These fellows were seen coming from a gap of the mountain, some distance off, making direct for our little party, who went out at full gallop to meet them. A discharge of arrows was met by a volley from our men. A considerable skirmish now ensued. The Indians, raising the war-whoop, rushed on them, discharging their arrows with incredible rapidity; but they were forced to retreat, and these bodies were dragged hither as trophies.

14th.—About one o'clock in the night, while our wearied soldiers slept, two guns were heard. In an instant our captain jumped to his feet, and hurriedly went over the ground to wake us all up. In a few moments every man had on his arms. After waiting some time for the enemy, news came that one of the lieutenants was shot through the hand. It appears that this lieutenant was officer of the night, and in his rounds tried to take a sentinel by surprise. Creeping stealthily on the ground to the spot, he was told by the sentinel to stop and give the countersign. No answer being returned, he tired. As soon as he found that he was shot in the hand, he returned the charge on the sentinel.

But no one can tell as yet who this watchful sentinel is. I made up a fire to prepare coffee. At two o'clock the reveille sounded for all to saddle up. At four we started, and after marching twenty-five miles, came in sight of Parras, a large city. Our Adjutant chose a place for us to encamp, which is the beautiful grove of ornamental cotton trees. The scene is new and pleasant. Here are trees, green cornfields, and running streams. The gardens in and around the city are beautifully arranged, and *tastefully* supplied with ripe apricots, oranges, and lemons; also a great variety of flowering shrubs and plants.

15th.—We are to pass a day or two here, I believe, resting from our long travel. This morning one of our wagon drivers, who is a sailor, went up town, and by some means, most unfortunately, offended several of the Mexican gentlemen. Complaint was made to the *alcade*, who ordered Jack to be taken to the *caliboose* and flogged, going in person to see it done. But Jack knocked him down and broke his sabre in pieces—whipping several others who came to the rescue, and finally walked off to camp completely victorious. Word was brought to Col. Doniphan about the conduct of this man, who gravely told the people that if Gen. Wool could do anything with his men, it was more than he could with his. He said it was now too late for him to keep them in order, therefore, he should leave on Monday.

Sunday, 16th.—Preparations are going on in different departments for the renewal of our march tomorrow. The expectation of soon encountering Generals Taylor and Wool, appears to inspire our men with a desire to look decent. Old clothes are being washed—sundry holes in deer skin pants are in the process of repair, and I think we shall not look so very ragged after all.

17th,—Moved out of town at three o'clock, p. m. After marching five miles through a broken, bare country, we came to a house, whose shingled roof indicated that its builder had been educated in the United States. We found it even so, although the man was a Mexican. We made a journey of twenty-five miles today, and had a supper of excessively tough beef, and coarse bread.

28th.— On our way, very early, as usual—made eighteen miles with a severe earache, from which I have suffered almost constantly for several weeks past. Strolling out after the tents were fixed up, I saw some soldiers walking along with a man in front, whom I learned they were about to drum out of service. He proved to be a teamster, and not a volunteer. He had, without provocation, struck several Mexicans in Parras. The *alcade* sending on an express to Gen. Wool for protection, induced Col. Doniphan to settle the business thus. He was made to walk before three armed men, behind whom several bugles performed a doleful ditty. When they arrived at the outskirts, the captain ordered a halt, and proclaimed that the man was drummed out of service for misbehaviour. Whereupon he ordered the men in front to kick him. The punishment having been inflicted, the poor fellow was turned off, to find shelter where he could.

11th.—Tonight we are encamped at a ranch, almost overflowed with water, which is coming down with a rush, in consequence of a heavy rain in the mountains. Made today twenty-five miles.

21st.—Yesterday and today we pursued our journey without intermission. At night we encamped where Gen. Wool had stationed 1000 men as picket guard. We received a treat in the shape of nice American flour and mess pork, as rations.

22nd.—I rode with several others to Gen. Wool s camp. On the way we passed over the battle ground of Buena Vista, and saw the remains of hundreds of Mexicans thrown in heaps, and covered over with cactus. These remained undisturbed by the wolves, while they had disinterred our Americans and devoured them; these animals make a practice in keeping in the rear of our advancing armies, and always prefer eating our men after death to the Mexicans. I spent an hour in contemplating the desolations of war-picked up a few Spanish coins, a watch key, cross &c. with several other little matters, as mementos. Gen. Wool's quarters were to be seen in the distance.

After spending an hour or two in camp, I returned to our boys, whom I found assembled in a congregation, and Capt. Reid holding forth in a speech, trying all his might, to get some of our men to volunteer again, their term being nearly expired. This morning every preparation is made for the reception of General Wool, who is expected to receive the command. All in right order, we marched out the artillery in front, our company, (the Chihuahua Rangers) next, and so on. As he rode up the artillerymen fired a salute, and while passing along the lines with his escort, we had orders to "present arms."

After the parade was over, we were marched back to camp, where the general came to inspect the captured cannon, and see the black flag, taken at the battle of Sacramento. At night we drew rations of bacon and dried apples, which good things, some of our boys thought were given as a *bribe* to induce them to re-enlist.

Sunday, 23rd.—We left at an early hour, and as we passed through Gen. Wool's encampment, we turned over to him our American artillery, consisting of six pieces, received at Santa Fe. We retained the Mexican cannon, *viz.* seventeen pieces taken at the battle of Sacramento, and one piece taken at Bracito, and marched on twelve miles to Saltillo, a large town among the mountains. The weather is warm and pleasant, and in right order we passed through, and proceeded on eight miles; we encamped at night in a wheat field. We saw today several deserted *ranchos*.

24th.—After a long and fatiguing march of thirty-two miles, we stopped at a deserted ranch to pass the night. In winding through the mountain passes today, we turned aside to see the fortifications which had been thrown up, to stop the progress of Gen. Taylor to Saltillo.

25th.—An early start and fatiguing journey of twenty-five miles, brought us within four miles of Monterey. From our camp we have a full view of the city and palace of the bishop. All this day our road lay through the narrow pass of the mountains, one of which is volcanic, and has been burning for several years. A heavy rain descended tonight, drenching us completely, and in the midst of which a grave was dug for a poor soldier, who has been sick ever since we left Chihuahua.

26th.— Through a heavy wind we rode into town, and stopped to see the citadel and wall so bravely scaled by our troops, after the enemy was driven from their redoubts. From this palace, a lovely and extensive view of the city and surrounding country is presented. The southern fruits and flowers are growing in great luxuriance. Alter our men were satisfied with an inspection, we marched through the famous town of Monterey to Gen. Taylor's camp, where we arrived at 12 o'clock. We found the old hero encamped in the woods. Immediately on our arrival he came to us, in company with Col. Doniphan, to see the trophies of our victories. I was fortunate enough to grasp the hand of the old general. In the afternoon several thousand pack mules were sent out with provisions for Gen. Wool.

27th.—At daybreak the roll-call was called, and Capt. Hudson told us to saddle up and get ready to start. All was in readiness, when orders came that we should be delayed till 12 o'clock. A few minutes before that hour, Gen. Taylor with his escort rode up, and passed along the lines, with his hat off, to review us. We presented sabres and then started on our way, the general escorting us some distance from his camp. After he left us, we pursued our march through a country well covered with hackberry and other trees. A long route of thirty-two miles brought us to a ranch, where we halted for the night.

28th.—Arrived at a deserted ranch late in the morning, after passing forty miles over a most dreadful road. Being in the rear guard, I and eleven others, were obliged to assist the wagons up the hills, by pushing at the wheels. All along this route decaying bodies and skeletons of men are lying. Some of the bodies still had their clothing on, and the stench was almost intolerable. The road was also strewed with mules, which had died in numbers on their way to Monterey.

29th.—The road is only interesting from association. Many a brave man has passed it never to retrace his steps. Six miles from our last stopping place, we reached Seralvo. Here we found a regiment of volunteers on the march to join General Taylor. We waited till the afternoon to feed our horses and mules; then marched fourteen miles to another deserted ranch, and stopped to sleep. We saw, on our way, many ranches and villages tenantless and destroyed. While we were at Seralvo, a Mexican was caught, who belonged to the gang that murdered the teamsters, and burned up 150 wagons, which were on their way to the army.

At three o'clock he was brought out in the *plaza,*; and placed against the wall. A file of six men, (the Texan Rangers,) stood some ten yards off. The prisoner was told by the colonel that his time was at hand. He was then ordered to turn his back. This he not only refused to do, but struck fire and lighted his cigar. The word was given—all fired—and he fell dead. Three balls entered his breast, and three his head. A Texan, whose brother had been murdered in the wagon train, gave a five dollar gold piece to take the place of one who was chosen to do this melancholy business.

Sunday night, 30th.—We have stopped at a town called Mier. I felt very weary after a travel of thirty-six miles. This place is notorious on account of a battle that was gained by the Texans. Our Rangers were highly elated in the thoughts of their success, and they became so drunk, that the defeated Mexicans took them prisoners, and marched them off to the city of Mexico. So much for the sale of rum. We met with a cordial reception at this place.

31st.—We encamped in sight of Camargo at two o'clock today. We crossed the River St. Pon in a ferry boat, which was pulled by means of ropes. The crossing occupied about two hours, when our troops and artillery were landed. This town is well fortified. It is the principal depot for supplies to the army, which come up this river in small steamers. River water is drank, although rendered very filthy by the carcasses of mules and horses, which are thrown into it. Today one poor fellow was buried, who had been sick a long time. Many a hard jolt in the rough wagon, and hour of thirst and weariness had he—but he sleeps quietly and peacefully in his lonely rest on the banks of the St. Pon.

June 1st.—On our way to the Rio Grande, this morning one of our men was shot by a party of Mexicans, who had concealed themselves in the bushes. He was riding alone, when he was fired upon. The charge entered his hand and breast, and he fell dead. Capt. Reid at the head of fifty men, went after the murderers, and soon returned with six of them. They are to be kept in close confinement.

2nd.—Our officers were in an unpleasant dilemma. They did not know how to dispose of the prisoners, and after some debate, they concluded to turn them loose. A file of soldiers was detailed for that purpose. They took them some miles off, and soon returned, announcing that *they had turned them loose.* At 4 o'clock we left, and travelled all night through a thick forest of *muskeet* trees and brushwood. About sunrise we arrived at Columbus, where we found several steamers ready for us. Many of us were miserably disordered from our weary midnight march. We encamped on the Rio Grande. This evening our cannon was sent down the river two miles to be shipped.

3rd.—Orders were received at an early hour for the troops to bring forward their saddles, rigging, &c., to be valued. A most unsightly mass was soon presented, as the dilapidated articles were gathered in a heap. Our sergeant gave notice he should value them as condemned property, it being impossible to transport them. A large fire was then made, and all were consumed. Our horses were placed in charge of a Mr. Van Bibber, who for a stipulated sum engaged to drive them through Texas to Missouri, and leave them at any point we might designate. We walked a mile to the beach, where several steamers awaited us. The sick went immediately on board. Two or three companies started, whilst the rest of us were detained till very late to assist in shipping the cannon. Orders were given that we should remain all night, so we went again on shore, spread our blankets on the beach, and spent the night rather uncomfortably.

4th.—It commenced raining at 3 o'clock this morning. After eating a breakfast of coffee and a few hard crackers, we hurried on board the steamer. Here we found both cabin and deck crowded with men. Our little steamer started in the midst of a heavy rain, rendering everything exceedingly unpleasant. Night came on and no cooking could be done, so we went on shore, erected our tents, ate our suppers, and rested quietly through the night.

5th.—The bell rang at 3 o'clock for us to come on board, which we accomplished in the course of an hour. One fellow being rather slow, was left behind, but he regained the boat before she had gone two miles. Fortunately for him an accident happened to the wheel, which was found to be broken, thus detaining us for repairs several hours. We did not reach Metamoras till two o'clock. Here we stopped but a very few minutes, and proceeded on till sunset. The boat now stopped to take in wood, and the captain informed us that he should leave at moonrise. We laid down on deck on our blankets.

Sunday, 6th.—I was awakened at one o'clock by the deck hands, to make room to haul in the foot plank. I found myself drenched with filthy water, which had run under me as I slept. Quietly folding up my blanket, I thought I would make no complaint, as I was near my journey's end. About sunrise we reached the Balize, when all hands landed and erected the tents. After breakfast, with a number of others, I went to bathe in the sea. We let the breakers pass over our heads. They came in such force, that in my present reduced state, I found it difficult to stand up under them. Nor could I remain long in the water.

7th.—We are encamped on the banks of the Rio Grande, eight miles from the shipping, which is on the opposite side of this narrow neck of land.

8th.—A regiment of regulars landed today, on, their way to the seat of war. No ship has appeared as yet to take us off.

9th.—This morning we had orders to start for Brazos Santiago, nine miles from this place. We had not proceeded far through the deep sand, when it became necessary to for those who had the remnant of shoes, to pull them off, on account of the sand gathering in them, it being above the ankle at every step. Our feet became badly blistered by the heat and friction. Most gladly did I spread my blanket on the sand and enjoy a night of rest, after the fatigues of the day. We are not yet at the end of this uncomfortable journey. The shipping is in sight, and a short march in the morning will relieve the weary teams of their burdens.

10th.—We are all on board—artillery, baggage, and a motley crew of 250 men, with unshaved faces, ragged and dirty, but all in fine spirits, save a few poor fellows, whose thin visages show the ravages of disease and suffering.

11th.—The past has been a memorable night. For suffering I have not experienced its equal in all my peregrinations through life. In the brig, on board of which we took passage, there were 100 bunks, (a slight elevation made of plank,) for the soldiers to sleep on. When I got in mine, the crowd was so great and the air so oppressive, that I thought I would get out and take a few pulls at the fresh atmosphere. Groping along in the dark, I endeavoured to find some place of egress, but the whole gangway was strewed with men, and I was forced to return, amid a shower of *blessings* from the poor fellows on whom I had the misfortune to tread, I laid the rest of the night in this hot place, more dead than alive. There was not the slightest air, and I was covered with a profuse perspiration.

12th.—An inspection of this brig, which was beautiful in its exterior, convinced me that it was a filthy place indeed; especially between decks. It was certainly worse than a hog-pen, for just above our bunks there was a sty, in which were several of the real material. Two small fires were built for the soldiers to cook with, and so many crowded around them, all anxious to be served, that a long time elapsed before I could get my coffee. As a matter of convenience we were supplied with hard crackers and molasses. This diet only increased my disease, and I turned a longing eye on a large turtle which had been killed, and was being served up for our officers and the inmates of the cabin.

13th.—Our allowance of water was a coffee pot full twice a day for coffee, and a pint a piece for each man to drink; a hogshead had been drawn upon deck for our use. There is a guard kept throughout each day, over this hogshead of miserable water, not fit for horses to drink. It was with mingled feelings of admiration and sorrow that I saw our brave fellows, who had borne the fatigues of the march, and the strong blows of the battle, come humbly around the hogshead, which was a central point of attraction, and ask for a little cup of water, when they were almost famished, and could drink several pints, were it allowed them. It is a gloomy Sabbath evening, nearly calm.

14th.—We are running S. E. by E., though the boat scarcely glides along, there being a calm. It seems that the water is becoming scarcer to-day. The captain has directed that a quart only shall be given to each man for all purposes. And it is to last twenty-four hours. When this was announced one of the men muttered something which I did not hear, but which the captain disliked; for he told us all, that if any one made another threat, he would blow his brains out as quick as he would shoot a rattlesnake. When this threat was heard, the men all roared out in a hearty laugh.

The captain was of middle size, somewhat corpulent, swarthy in complexion, and blind in his right eye. He was rough in his manners, but talked very little, especially to us privates. He is master of the brig, and is employed by government to convey troops across the gulf. His name is Woodsides. This morning about a pint of water was issued to each man. Of course, no coffee is made. We mixed a little vinegar with some water, and with crackers and molasses, made out our supper. Two dolphins were caught by the sailors, and one of our men caught a young shark. Another turtle is served up for the cabin, it was so warm that I could not sleep in my bunk, but lay in the gangway, on my blanket. At midnight a steamer came alongside, and the captain took on board several barrels of water. It was truly a blessing for us.

15th.—Coffee and fried shark for breakfast, but a dreadful sore mouth, (which I fear is the scurvy,) makes the eating a painful performance. Every indication of land was near. At 12 o'clock the captain said we were eighty miles from the Balize. In anticipation of a storm, the sails were furled, but a little sprinkle of rain was all, and we again spread our canvass to the breeze. A sailor was sent aloft to see if the light house was in sight, and after remaining in the cross trees two hours, he came down and said he saw it. A short time after the cry was heard, "the pilot boat is coming." Sails were furled, and the pilot was soon on board. In the meantime someone cried "three cheers for Capt. Woodsides!" The cry was echoed by the crowd, and Capt. Woodsides looked bullets.

A flag was placed on the bow, a steamer came alongside and towed us over the bar, where our captain anchored. We now draw water up the sides of the ship, for we are in the Mississippi River, 100 miles from New Orleans. The water is good and there is plenty of it, as the river is full. Every man has just as much as he can use, and we use it freely enough. After supper I went to my bunk, but found it too warm to rest in, so I took my blanket, and laid down as usual, in the gangway, but not being able to stretch my feet out, in consequence of a sack of bacon in the way, I got up and searched about, and at length found an empty bunk of someone who had gone on deck to spend the night. I felt weak and sick from the heat.

16th.—We drew our water from the river to get some breakfast; the sailors are washing off the deck, and if any man happens in the way, he is sure of having a bucket full thrown on him; of course several of our boys have had a good drenching. At 8 o'clock a steamer took us tow. As we proceeded up the Mississippi, we beheld on its banks large plantations of the sugar cane, which present a lovely contrast with some countries over which I have marched. On the left side of the river is Fort Jackson, now nearly in ruins, but still a beautiful place. With several of our men I slept on the deck of the steamer. We were all in good spirits at the prospect of getting home, though the want of a change of clothes at this particular juncture is keenly felt. Some are covered with filth and vermin, which have kept their hiding places within our garments for many a long day.

17th.—We are now among the thick settlements and sugar plantations which line the river as we approach the city. I remained most of the night on deck, and ate an early breakfast of the usual diet. Afterwards Capt. Hudson had one of his big guns taken up, and tired a salute as we passed a pretty little village. We are now on the site of the battle ground, where General Jackson fought the English in 1814—continued our course up the river, and fired several times. At last, we were safely landed on the wharf in New Orleans.

Upon my head there was no hat, having lost my last remnant overboard in the Gulf. My pants I had thrown away three days before, because (being composed of deerskin, worn into tatters,) I despaired of making them look decent. A pair of drawers, rather the worse for wear, and an old overcoat, constituted my dress. If, to this description of my person I add that my hair, beard, and mustachios, had been left to vegetate undisturbed ever since I left Fort Leavenworth, then some idea may be formed of the accomplished soldiers of Col. Doniphan's command.

18th.—In company with twelve others, I got in an omnibus to search for some clothes and quarters; came three miles to a large clothing establishment, where our wants as to garments were soon supplied. The barber next exercised his skill, and it was with many an amusing jest and laugh that we regarded each others' altered and improved appearance. Comfortable quarters were secured, and tonight I am reposing in a quiet boarding house. Here I feel that no homage of my soul is profound enough to render due adoration to that gracious Providence who has protected and guided me, while marching over the wild plains, and through the mountain passes of Mexico.

Deserts in vain opposed our onward course;
O'er hostile lands and wild untravelled wastes.
Our journey we pursued, nor feared the floods,
Through deep ravines that flow; dire banked with death;
Nor mountains in whose jaws destruction grinned.
Though floods rapacious roaring as they rolled.
And mountains huge and rough were circled round
By roving bands of restless savage foes.

22nd.—On Sunday last I went to the M. E. Church and listened to an excellent sermon. I was kindly invited by a stranger, who introduced himself to me, to dine and spend the evening with him. I complied with his request, and was pleasantly entertained. After tea I returned to my boarding house, which is kept by a Mr. Wren, and whose charge is moderate, *viz.* $4 per week. On my first introduction here I committed a blunder, the thought of which has frequently caused me to smile. It shows the contrast between a camp life and the more polished proceedings of life in the city. When I was called to the first meal, I seated myself at the table in the presence of my hostess, and commenced operations as I supposed in a manner the most polite and refined.

Casting a glance at the lady, I observed that she was eyeing me with a curious interest. The smile that played upon her lip, told me that she was amused at some awkwardness of mine, or some oddity in my appearance. And what was my surprise when I found that I had jerked my old knife from my pocket, and was cutting my meat placed upon my bread in the usual way. The habit had been fixed upon me, and notwithstanding the neat arrangements of the table, I could not resist the propensity to indulge in my camp customs.

26th.—On board the steamer *Louisville*, bound for Cincinnati. The boat is crowded, but a mattress on which to lie is a luxury. A few hours ago, I parted with many of my fellow soldiers and friends, with feelings which it is impossible for me to describe. I am not in a situation to continue with the regiment until it reaches its final destination. My mouth is so sore that the least effort to masticate my food is very painful, and I cannot eat, now that I have before me all the luxuries of life; and even if I could, it would be improper for me to do so, on account of a long continued diarrhoea and pain in my breast and side.

I feel that I am greatly changed, when I compare the present with the time when I last glided over this beautiful stream. Then so full of health and anticipations of pleasures and happiness, now, a sick soldier—a mere skeleton of a man, bronzed by the burning rays of a Mexican sun, and worn down by the prolonged fatigue of travelling, watching and toil. I regret very much that I cannot go to St. Louis, as requested by Colonel Doniphan, where an enthusiastic reception is awaiting him. To express myself in *measured terms* about our commander, would not be expressive of my feelings, and I feel how utterly incompetent I am to utter his eulogy.

The man who can familiarise himself with the poorest private, by some kind word, or ride among the troops, and make us forget that we were hungry or thirsty, by some pleasant converse, in our long and toilsome march;—the man who can forget his own personal safety in the hour of danger, and rise superior to every embarrassment—who can be prepared for every emergency, by superior skill in the tactics of war—as well as a refined sense of honour, and an open suavity of manner, not only leading captive the hearts of his entire command, but the thousands of the hostile foe—such a man is a treasure to society, an honour to his country. And, such a man, is the brave Doniphan. It was with the feelings of a brother or a friend to whom I owed many obligations, that I grasped the hand of this great man, who kindly wished me a safe return to my family.

27th.—Our noble steamer has made good headway up the river, passed Baton Rouge, and at nine o'clock at night came in sight of Natchez.

28th.—Passed the Grand Gulf at 10, and at 2 got to Vicksburg. The pleasure of feasting my eyes on scenes so lovely, and which are presented by a trip to the "Father of Waters," compensates for any little inconvenience arising from our crowded state.

30th.—At this time we are near Memphis. There is some excitement on board A man labouring under the effect of *mania potu* is quite crazy, and has attempted several times to jump overboard. Just now he entered the ladies' cabin and struck his wife; one of our officers interfered, and soon placed him on his back. But a further attempt to kill his child made it necessary to secure him. With several others I entered the ladies' cabin, and helped to tie this *gentleman*. He made much useless resistance.

July 1st.—Slept but little—the surrounding bustle and noise mingled strangely with dreamy anticipations of soon receiving the cordial welcome of friends, that I fondly think are eagerly awaiting me in my native home.

West River, July 10th.—Let no brave soldier say he cannot shed tears of joy, when clasped in the arms of his aged mother, after an absence of nearly two years, in which he has encountered the perils of both land and sea—travelling nearly 6000 miles, 2200 being through the heart of an enemy's country, and witnessing death in every shape and feature.

It were an endless task to attempt anything like a minute description of that part of Mexico through which we travelled. Our route lay for the most part on the Rio Grande del Norte, whose head waters rise in the Green Mountains, several hundred miles above Santa Fe. It forms the water boundary of Texas, and can be easily forded at almost any point above El Passo. In the dry season it is extremely low, and can be of very little importance for navigation, except near its mouth which flows into the Gulf of Mexico.

It is thought this river has a course of from 15 to 1800 miles. The country is elevated, being traversed by a range of mountains extending far to the northward. Among the inhabitants, I saw every shade of complexion, from a dark swarthy, or yellow, to the palest white. But few are handsome among the ladies; and this is principally to be attributed to their great love of colouring the skin with red paint. The mountaineers are mostly poor, and almost universally destitute of everything beyond the bare necessaries of life Their flocks and herds constitute their principal riches and their implements of husbandry, are all of the most simple character.

Their ploughing such as it is, is effected by a wooden plough, to which is attached two or four oxen, and the wheat is slightly covered over, having been previously sown on the hard ground. There are some fertile valleys in this mountainous range but the poor simple inhabitants have very little idea of taking advantage of the natural resources of their country. After we left Chihuahua, fields of cotton and corn interspersed at intervals with the sugarcane, presented themselves.

The *ranchos* are always about a day's journey apart, and the whole aspect of nature in these delightful spots is one of the most inviting that can be imagined as a field of operation for the industry and art of man. The sod here is fertile, and what is generally termed bottom land,

and with proper culture would be as productive as any of our western lands, as the climate is more genial. They grow only a few vegetables, of which the red pepper appears to be a favourite; these they string and hang on the outsides of their houses so thick that on approaching I frequently thought I should see a painted dwelling, but was to see only a miserable dirty hut.

The mines of Mexico afford her principal wealth, but of this the poorer classes obtain but little; they are kept in ignorance and degradation by a government which has borne the name of Republican, but which everyone who sojourns in that country must soon discover to be a mockery for the mass of the people are subject alone to the will of the Roman clergy, and are not free to act. There is no slave in any of our Southern States whose situation they have not reason to envy.

The women are more degraded u possible than the men; and more slovenly in their appearance and while this is the case in any country, the morals of the people must remain at a low grade. Since my return I have heard of the enthusiastic reception of Col. Doniphan at St. Louis, an account of which I annex as published in the *Baltimore American*. Our business was not, however, to see all that was worth seeing, but to hurry on to the place we started for, and when arrived at that, to make arrangements to hurry on again.

Col. Doniphan's March

At the recent reception of the Missouri volunteers under Col. Doniphan at St. Louis, the address of welcome was delivered by Mr. Senator Benton. The speech is characteristic—exhibiting that clear and graphic narrative, and those strong and concentrated expressions for which the Senator is remarkable.

The orator gave an outline of the long march of this gallant regiment—first, a thousand miles to New Mexico, which became a starting point of a new departure. Then Chihuahua was aimed at—Chihuahua, a rich and populous city of nearly thirty thousand souls, the seat of the government of the state of that name, and formerly the residence of the Captains General of the Internal Provinces under the vice-regal government. In advancing towards Chihuahua the adventurous regiment encountered incredible hardships.

They passed over the desert called *et jornada de los muertos*—the journey of the dead—an arid plain of ninety miles strewed with the bones of animals perished of hunger and thirst, and marked by continual mementos of men who had fallen victims to the perilous way. They fought the enemy at the Bracito, and gained a decisive victory, although opposed by superior numbers, strong in cavalry and artillery. Again at Sacramento the intrepid band fought and conquered a vastly superior force, Mr. Benton calls that victory "one of the military marvels of the age." At length Chihuahua is reached and taken, and there the bold adventurers must pause to determine which way next they shall direct their steps. They had occupied a city about as far from St. Louis as Moscow is from Paris, Let Col. Benton's graphic narrative be heard:

Chihuahua gained, it became, like Santa Fe, not the terminating point of a long expedition, but the beginning point of a new one. General Taylor was somewhere—no one knew exactly where—but some seven or eight hundred miles towards the other side of Mexico. You heard that he had been defeated—that *Buena Vista* had not been a *good prospect* to him. Like good Americans you did not believe a word of it; but like good soldiers, you thought it best to go and see.

A volunteer party of fourteen, headed by Collins of Boonville, undertake to penetrate to Saltillo, and to bring you information of his condition. They set out. Amidst innumerable dangers they accomplish their purpose, and return. You march. A vanguard of one hundred men, led by Lieut. Colonel Mitchell, led the way. Then came the main body, (if the name is not a *burlesque* on such a handful,) commanded by Col. Doniphan himself.

The whole table land of Mexico, in all its breadth, from west to east, was to be traversed. A numerous and hostile population in towns—treacherous Comanches in the mountains—were to be passed. Everything was to be self-provided— provisions, transportation, fresh horses for remounts, and even the means of victory—and all without a military chest, or even an empty box, in which government gold had ever reposed. All was accomplished. Mexican towns were passed, in order and quiet: plundering Comanches punished: means were obtained from traders to liquidate indispensible contributions: and the wants that could not be supplied, were endured like soldiers of veteran service.

I say the Comanches were punished. And here presents itself an episode of a novel, extraordinary, and romantic kind— Americans chastising savages for plundering people who they themselves came to conquer, and forcing the restitution of captives and of plundered property. A strange story this to tell in Europe, where back-woods character, western character is not yet completely known. But to the facts. In the *muskeet* forest of the *Bolson de Mapimi*, in the *sierras* around the beautiful town and fertile district of Parras, and in all the open country for hundreds of miles round about, the savage Camanches have held dominion ever since the usurper Santa Anna disarmed the people; and sally forth from their fastnesses to slaughter men, plunder cattle, and carry off women and children.

An exploit of this kind had just been performed on the line of the Missourians' march, not far from Parras, and an advanced party chanced to be in that town at the time the news of the depredation arrived there. It was only fifteen strong. Moved by gratitude for the kind attentions of the people, especially the women, to the sick of General Wool's command, necessarily left in Parras, and unwilling to be outdone by enemies in generosity, the heroic fifteen, upon the spot, volunteered to go back, hunt out the depredators, and punish them, without regard to numbers. A grateful Mexican became their guide. On their way they fell in with fifteen more of their comrades; and, in short time, seventeen Camanches killed out of sixty-five, eighteen captives restored to their families, and three hundred and fifty head of cattle recovered for their owners, was the fruit of this sudden and romantic episode.

Such noble conduct was not without its effect on the minds of the astonished Mexicans. An official document from the Prefect of the place to Captain Reid, leader of this detachment, attests the verity of the fact, and the gratitude of the Mexicans; and constitutes a trophy of a new kind in the annals of war. Here it is in the original Spanish, and I will read it off in English.

It is officially dated from the Prefecture of the Department of Parras, signed by the Prefect Jose Ignacio Arrabe. and addressed to Captain Raid, the 18th of May, and says:

'At the first notice that the barbarians, after killing many, and taking captives, were returning to their haunts, you generously and bravely offered, with fifteen of your subordinates, to fight them on their crossing by the Pozo, executing this enterprise with celerity, address and bravely worthy of all eulogy, and worthy of the brilliant issue which all celebrate. You recovered many animals and much plundered property; and eighteen captives were restored to liberty and to social enjoyment, their souls overflowing with a lively sentiment of joy and gratitude, which all the inhabitants of this town equally breathe, in favour of their generous deliverers and their valiant chief. The half of the Indians killed in the combat, and those which fly wounded, do not calm the pain which all feel for the wound which your Excellency received defending Christians and civilized beings against the rage and brutality of savages. All desire the speedy re-establishment of your health; and although they know that in your own noble soul will be found the best reward of your con-

83

duct, they desire also to address you the expression of their gratitude and high esteem. I am honoured in being the organ of the public sentiment, and pray you to accept it, with the assurance of my most distinguished esteem. God and Liberty!'

This is a trophy of a new kind in war, won by thirty Missourians, and worthy to be held up to the admiration of Christendom.

The regiment arrived at Gen. Taylor's camp at Monterey, and reported themselves ready for duty. They were prepared to go with the hero of Buena Vista to San Luis Potosi, or Zacatecas, or the city of Mexico. They regarded not their fatigues nor the approaching expiration of their term of service.

"But unhappily," says Mr. Benton, "the conqueror of Palo Alto, Resaca de la Palma, Monterey and Buena Vista, was not exactly in the condition that the Lieutenant General, might have been, intended him to be. He was not at the head of 20,000 men! he was not at the head of any thousands that would enable him to march! and had he to decline the proffered service. Thus the long marched and well fought volunteers—the rough, the ready, and the ragged—had to turn their faces towards home, still more than two thousand miles distant."

The last nine hundred miles of the land march from Chihuahua to Matamoras was made in forty-five days, with seventeen pieces of artillery, eleven of which had been taken from the enemy. During all their long march his regiment of hardy soldiers received from the Government not a dollar of pay; they furnished for the most part their own supplies and forage and clothing, and yet brought back nearly their whole number. "You marched farther than the farthest," says Mr. Benton, "you have fought as well as the best, left order and quiet in your train, and lost less money than any."

Col. Doniphan made an eloquent address in reply to the oration of welcome, and towards the close of it, he turned to his men, the companions of his toils and dangers, and said:

You have endured much toil and hardship. It is now about to terminate. You have arrived once more in the land of civilized society, and again we are citizens mingling with our fellow-citizens. Your lot has been a hard one in many respects.

Before reaching New Mexico, by two hundred miles, you were on half rations, and never afterwards, for a single day, during our long and arduous march to Saltillo, did you receive full rations. Yet all this you have borne, and you have borne it with fortitude. The order which you received to march in Major Gilpin's command, with a large column, over the Sierra Madre, covered with perpetual snow—proceeding on your march on shortened allowance, without tents or transportation, and many other comforts, because the Government was unable to furnish them; yet you bore it all, and were ready to resume your march in two days on the city of Chihuahua. You have travelled over five states of Mexico, and five very large ones, in point of territory.

Perhaps the citizens of St. Louis do not know what a *Bonava* is, but I will answer for every man in my command, knowing what they are. I may assure you, had you crossed them, you, too, would have known what they are. The shortest one that we crossed, was fifty miles, and one ninety-five miles, which we crossed in three days in December, without wood, without water, without tents, at an elevation of 7000 feet above the Atlantic Ocean. In sending expresses to the distance of 600 miles, when I was unable to furnish them with the means of carrying provision and other comfort with them over immense sand prairies, covered with snow, I have never made a detail, but all were volunteers, or when I have sent out parties for the purpose of watching the enemy, who have had to starve for days, I never made a detail in this column, but all were volunteers, and I am proud to say it.

A Sketch of the Life and Character of Col. Alexander W. Doniphan

By D. C. Allen

Preface

On December 7th. 1895, I read before the Kansas City Bar Association, by its imitation, the *Sketch of the Life and Character of Col. Alexander W. Doniphan* which follows these words of preface. It appeared in the issue for January, 1896. of the *Kansas City Bar Monthly*.

At a recent meeting of the survivors of Company C, 1st Regiment of Missouri Mounted Volunteers, in the Mexican War, who reside in Clay Co., Mo., they decided to give the *Sketch* some greater certainty of preservation by having a number of copies of it printed in pamphlet form and strongly bound) and depositing three copies of it in each of the College, University and public libraries of Missouri. They decided, also, that a preface should be given to the *Sketch*, containing the roster of Company C with a few explanatory remarks. For the gratification of themselves and those into whose hands the pamphlets may fall, they concluded, in addition, to add to the *Sketch* pictures of the Captain of Company C and of Col. Doniphan. The execution of their purpose they placed on me. It is a work of pleasure. The names of the members of Company C, mustered into the service of the United States at Fort Leavenworth June 7th, 1846, are as follow:

Officers:—Oliver Perry Moss, Captain: Linneus Bowlin Sublette, 1st, James H. Moss, 2nd, and Henry Thomas Ogden, 3rd Lieutenant; James H. Long. Thomas McCarty, William Wallis and Adam K. McClintock, Sergeants; William Carroll Skaggs, George Henry Wallis, John S. Groom and Martin Cloud, Corporals; and Abraham Estes, Bugler, and James Barnes, Blacksmith.

Privates:—Henry B. Ammons, Parker Benthal, John Briscoe, William Beale, James Burns, George W. Bell, E. W. Burton. Allen Cox, Rufus R. Cox, James P. Cooper, Smith Cummins, George W. Crowley, John G. Christy, James Chorn, Edwin W. Crapster, William C. Campbell, Hiram Chaney, Noah Paley Carpenter, Simon Hudson Clayton,

Alexander W. Doniphan, Washington W. Drew, James Harvey Darnall, Theodore Duncan, Matthew Duncan, William Duncan, Benjamin Riley, Everett Henry Ellis, Havey W. English, Spencer Faubion, James A. Finley, Levi Franklin, William R. Franklin, Thomas J. Fealand, Robert W. Fleming, George Fleming, William C. Gunter, Hiram Green, Charles Human, John D. Holt, Francis Carroll Hughes, John T. Hughes, Alexander Hall (known as Dock Hall), Willard P. Hall, James Hall, Newton H. Jacobs, Baylor Jacobs, Andrew Job, Joseph Letchworth, William T. Lard, John P. Lard, James Lamar, Southey R. Long, Richardson Long, Benjamin W. Marsh, Solomon McNeese, Albert McQuiddy, Wesley Martin, Eli Murray. DeWilton Mosby, James McGee, Abraham Miller, James F. Morton, John James Moore, Richard A. Neeley, John Nash, John Neal, Edward Owens, Jesse L. Price, Josiah Pence, William H. Pence. Peter C. Pixlee, William C. Patterson, Benjamin Pendleton, Nimrod Pendergrass, John K. Rollins, Charles F. Ruff, William H. Russell, Martin Ringo, Alonzo F. Rudd, Robert Shearer, John W. Shouse, Riley Stoutt, Obediah Sullivan, John S. Story, James R. Sites, Alexander Cunningham Scott, James Sanders, Robert Thomas Stephenson, Joseph Sanderson, Joseph Addison Smith, Chilton B. Samuel, W. P. A. Snowden, Joshua B. Tillery, Andrew W. Tracey, William A. Thompson, Thomas Waller, William Wells, Hardin Warren, John Warren, Gideon Wood, James A. Wills, James N. York, and John York. To these I add Jake Laidlaw, Capt. Moss negro servant.

With the exception of Willard P. Hall, Company C, containing; 118 men, rank and file, was wholly composed of volunteers from Clay County. He took the place of a volunteer who was discharged from service, through the intervention of his father, because of minority. Willard P. Hall was afterwards a member of Congress, and, subsequently, Governor of Missouri. As is known, Alexander W. Doniphan was elected Colonel and Charles F. Ruff Lieutenant-Colonel of the 1st Regiment. Parker Benthall became so severely ill at Fort Leavenworth that he was unable to proceed with his company.

The pictures of Col. Doniphan and Capt. Moss, accompanying this *Sketch*, are very life-like as all will bear witness who knew them. That of Col. Doniphan is from a photograph taken in May, 1879, when he was, for him, in excellent health, and before the shrinkage of old age had begun. His expression was always extremely difficult for the artist to catch, but the photograph mentioned comes nearer to the seizure and nearer to showing us the real man than any picture of him I ever saw.

So far as I know, there does not exist in print or manuscript, outside of the accompanying *Sketch*, (beyond a few phrases of compliment in very meagre biographical accounts of him, any estimate of the moral character and intellectual grandeur of Col. Doniphan. Mine is an attempt,—feeble and imperfect,—to rescue from the unwritten past and give to the future, for the benefit, at least, of Missourians, some conception of that great man's personality and genius. I do this in the earnest hope that it may serve as a core around which some man of taste, ability and literary leisure may build a biographical monument worthy of the splendid qualities of our great Missourian.

D. C Allen.

Liberty, Mo., July 3rd, 1897.

Oliver Perry Moss

Col. Alexander W. Doniphan—
His Life and Character

Alexander William Doniphan was born in Mason county, Kentucky July 9. 1808. His father, Joseph Doniphan, was a native of King George, and his mother of Fauquier county, Virginia. His mother's maiden name was Anne Smith, and her paternal ancestor was among the original colonists at Jamestown, Virginia, in 1607. His first ancestor in America of the name of Doniphan, came from England to Virginia near the middle or latter part of the 17th century, and settled near what is known as the Northern Neck. The given name of that ancestor was Mott.

It is a tradition in the Doniphan family (a tradition which I neither avouch nor deny) traceable and fully believed by its members for more than a century, that it is of Spanish origin. According to the tradition, their ancestor, who separated from the parent stock in Spain, was a young Castilian, of noble blood, who served under Ferdinand and Isabella in the conquest of Granada, and was knighted by King Ferdinand for gallantry on the field. Afterward and during middle life he indicated a preference for Protestantism, and to escape the terrors of the Inquisition and enjoy the freedom of religious belief, he abandoned his native land and took refuge in England. There he married an English lady named Mott and from that union have descended the Doniphans of America.

The name—so speaks the tradition—of the young cavalier was Don Alfonso. This name, in English use, was insensibly corrupted into Doniphan.[1]

A lineage which is traceable to the chivalry of the battle field and the highest devotion to conviction, will always command the respect

---

1. So says the tradition.

ALEXANDER W. DONIPHAN

and admiration of men. The seven hundred years of battle between the Spaniards and Moors left the impress of supreme courage, undoubting faith and unconquerable will on the former, which easily made of them the foremost men of all Christendom four centuries ago. Perhaps the tradition is true. If so, I can explain without looking further, the tinge of old romance in Col. Doniphan's character, his wonderfully delicate respect for women, and his stern adherence to sentiments of honour; as if he were bound to these things—

By the dead gaze of all his ancestors:
And by the mystery of his Spanish blood,
Charged with the awe and glories of the past.

All of the members of the Smith and Doniphan families in Virginia were Whigs during our Revolutionary War, and those families contributed an unusually large proportion of their men to the Continental army. Joseph Doniphan was with Washington at Yorktown, and his brother, George Doniphan, died for freedom at Brandywine.

Joseph Doniphan had gone to Kentucky prior to 1779 and remained there a year or more. While there he was engaged in teaching school, and he was the first man "who taught the young idea haw to shoot" on the "Dark and Bloody Ground." Returning to Virginia prior to the siege of Yorktown, he entered the Continental army and remained in it until the conclusion of the revolutionary struggle. Marrying Anne Smith, he returned to Kentucky in 1790, and made his home in Mason county. Miss Smith was a lady of extraordinary mental powers and brilliant wit. She was an aunt, I may add, of the late Gov. William Smith of Virginia.

Joseph Doniphan was for a great many years prior to his death, the intimate friend of the famous Simon Kenton. It will be seen, therefore, that the subject of this sketch was born during the generation immediately succeeding the conclusion of the struggle for independence by the colonies and the wresting of the soil of Kentucky from the savages. He was born amid the odours of the forest. The first tales poured into his ears when he was old enough to be intelligent, were those of stern conflicts for liberty and civilisation. The first names by him lisped were those of Washington, Wayne, Marion. Lighthorse Harry Lee. and the whole immortal host of the Revolution. He was born when American manhood was at its acme, and the same profound feeling of patriotism thrilled every bosom from the Atlantic coast to the deepest recesses of the Western wilderness.

Joseph Doniphan died in the year 1813, and the subject of this sketch was left to the watchcare of his mother. She was adequate to the rearing of the young eaglet. At the age of eight years she placed him under the instruction of Richard Keene, of Augusta, Kentucky, a learned though eccentric Irishman, who was a graduate of Trinity College, Dublin. Mr. Keene was of that very considerable body of educated Irishment—ardent followers of Robert Emmet—who found their safety in emigration to America at the conclusion of the Irish Rebellion in 1798. Ardent, enthusiastic, boiling with courage, entertaining the most romantic ideas of freedom, they were a dynamical process in the history of every young mind brought in contact with them. An examination into the family history of our country will develop the fact that these young Irish teachers were an intellectual power and blessing all over the then settled portion of the United States. Col. Doniphan never ceased the expression of his gratitude to Mr. Keene.

One who was familiar with the absolute ease and accuracy with which Col. Doniphan wreaked his thoughts upon expression would he astonished at the declaration that he ever lacked for words. He said, however, that in his youth his vocabulary was limited and his expression clumsy and difficult. Mr. Keene assured him that only through acquaintance with the great poets could exact, powerful, brilliant expression be acquired. Through knowledge, said he, of the poets could alone come the precise meaning of words, the perfect pronunciation of them, the melody of speech. and the majestic declamation of the orator. By Mr. Keene's advice he carefully studied the poets, and results in the pupil went very far to prove correct the theory of the master.

At the age of fourteen years, he was entered a student at Augusta College, in Bracken county, Kentucky. For many years it was an institution of very high repute, but, as I understand. it has not been in existence for quite a length of time. He graduated there at the early age of eighteen years, with great distinction, particularly in the classics. While at Augusta College, he had the benefit of the training and moulding influences of several very able instructors. I mention, as being among them. Drs. Durbin and Bascom. He constantly through life expressed his deep sense of obligation to those two gentlemen. Dr. Durbin was a very accomplished man—suave and refined and was the author of a scholarly and elegant book of travels in the Levant. Dr. Bascom was, in his day, the greatest pulpit orator in the Union.

Though a Methodist in creed, the stern theology of John Knox was much nearer his nature. In the time of Cromwell he would have been a Fifth-Monarchy man. He was ever as if in his great Task Master's eye. He seemed to hear the last trumpet and to see the smoke of the Pit ascending forever and forever. Sixty years ago *Young's Night Thoughts*, a book now unread, was on every parlour table. Dr. Bascom seemed to have absorbed its profound melancholy. There were in his eloquence a sombre magnificence and a distant roar as if of the gathering storm. In Dr. Durbin Col. Doniphan admired the man and loved the friend, but in Dr. Bascom he saw the orator and felt his seizure upon the soul.

A reading of the sermons of Dr. Bascom will show that his influence on the pupil was greater and more lasting than that of Dr. Durbin. It is true that in Col. Doniphan's oratory there was nothing gloomy. There was often, however, a severe magnificence which could claim kinship with the terrors which peopled the imagination of Dr. Bascom. There were times in that oratory when men felt as if they lay helpless on some lofty, naked peak, where the lightnings flashed in their midst and the thunders rolled around them.

In lingering thus on the teachers of Col. Doniphan, it is because I clearly recognise the influence through life of an able teacher on his pupils, and for the further reason that he himself most distinctly saw and appreciated it. Besides, all men are, in a way, chameleons, and take on colour from their environments.

In his youth the predilection of Col. Doniphan was for the law as a life-profession, and this was largely through the influence of his mother, who was a woman of great and far-reaching mind. Upon quitting college, therefore, for the purpose of legal study, he entered the law-office of the Hon. Martin P. Marshall, of Augusta, Kentucky. In the opinion of the pupil, his legal preceptor was one of the most learned and able of all the members of the famous Marshall family. In the course of study recommended by Mr. Marshall and required by him of his pupil is to be discovered the first instance within my knowledge, in this country, of the strictly historical method in the study of the law. First of all he required his pupil to read and carefully study portions of the classical authors of the English language. In this occupation he expended six months.

It was, as Mr. Marshall phrased it, to fructify and chasten the pupil's imagination and give him wings for more arduous flights. Secondly, he required him to read the histories of England and America and cognate works so that he might see, historically, the evolution of our system of law. An, thirdly, he required of him a most careful study of those text-books of the law which were then considered necessary in order to admission to practice. These studies consumed near three years, and were under the eye of and with recitations to the preceptor. The progress of the pupil was great; and where the preceptor is learned and skilful and the pupil brilliant, we must measure progress in study by genius and not by time.

Towards the close of the year 1829 Col. Doniphan was licensed to practice law in the states of Kentucky and Ohio. In March. 1830, he immigrated to Missouri, and in the fore part of April of that year he was licensed to practice in this state by our Supreme Court, then in session at Fayette, in Howard county. On April 19, 1830, he made his home at Lexington, Missouri, and was enrolled a member of the Lexington bar on the 26th of the July succeeding. He became at once, heart and soul, a Missourian, and ever after so remained.

It was at Lexington, therefore, he began his long, successful and brilliant legal career. The practice of the law was then in the West far more laborious than it is now. Law libraries were few and limited, and the day of legal blanks had not arrived. At the age of twenty-two he was placed in collision with Abiel Leonard, Robert W. Wells. Peyton R. Hayden and others; gentlemen eminent for ability and legal attainments, all of them much older than he, and already expert in the management of causes. His maiden speech at the bar was made in 1830, and in defence of a man indicted for murder. He assisted Mr. Leonard. This was the first trial for murder that he had ever witnessed. His conduct in this trial was modest, and gave clear evidence of the dawning of the reputation as a criminal lawyer which he very soon afterward acquired.

In 1833 he removed to Liberty, Missouri, where he made his home for the succeeding thirty years. There he found, already established in the practice, those eminent lawyers, David R. Atchison, Amos Rees, James M. Hughes and Gen. Andrew S. Hughes. His experience at Lexington had been preparatory; at Liberty his reputation attained its zenith. Nor was the state of society there at the time unfavourable to the development of any of the manly, social or mental qualities.

I feel sure that I will be excused if, in the briefest manner, I rend the veil of the past and portray—imperfectly indeed—the environment, characteristics, origin, condition and social life of the men and women of Liberty and Clay County sixty-five years ago. From the standpoint of art, such a portrayal is germane to my subject. Every picture should have its background. The facts stated by me, when not taken from records, and all the opinions expressed, were derived from the distinguished gentleman whose life and character I am feebly sketching, or from other lips, yet older than his, whose accuracy and truth were beyond all doubt. Clay County was organised in 1822, and reduced to its present limits in 1833. Settlements began there in 1819 and the immigration constantly increased in number for five or six years thereafter. In 1830 its population was 5,338, which was, in the main, located on the territory comprised in its present area. Hence, in 1830, the county was not a wilderness. The population, drawn from Virginia, North Carolina, Tennessee, Kentucky, Maryland, and in lesser numbers from the other states, was purely of American birth. The customs, manners and modes of thought of colonial days still prevailed to a very marked degree. The influence of old, well-known, leading families was strong. In the larger proportion of cases public offices were filled from the ranks of the men of the higher classes.

For instance, its first circuit clerk was William L. Smith, a man of education and a gentleman of distinguished bearing and princely elegance of manners. Population emigrated in those days by families in a much larger degree than now. A man of wealth in the older states would emigrate west, bringing with him not only his family, but all his movable property—his flocks and herds, his men servants and maid servants. Some locality in Virginia or elsewhere would be almost exactly reproduced in Clay County. That was prior to the acerbities in political feeling which developed into civil war. It was immaterial from what state in the Union a man came. All were sons of the sires of the Revolution, kinsmen of the heroes of New Orleans and Lundy's Lane—all were Americans—and universal good feeling and brotherhood prevailed.

Several of the chief men of the county were from the East. Of the leading merchants of Liberty at that time, one, Cyrus Curtis, was from New York, and another, Hiram Rich, was from Vermont. Liberty was a little village of a couple of hundreds of inhabitants, but its business was enormous and ramified all over northwest Missouri. The business and leading men of town and county were beyond the average in capacity. They were generally young men, of high social station in their native localities, educated, chivalric, generous, and had come to the Far West—the verge of civilisation to make their homes and fortunes. The county was, indeed, on the verge of civilization. From its borders the explorer could track his uncertain and dangerous route only through the domains of savages, who were as fierce and terrible as their ancestors a thousand years ago, until his halting and feeble steps were checked by the roar of the waves beating on the western coast of America.

For the little town of Liberty, almost a hamlet then, a fortunate circumstance occurred. In 1827 the post of Fort Leavenworth was established. At that post there always has been a greater accumulation of troops than at any other in the Union. Liberty was the nearest town to it. To relieve the tedium of station life there resorted to Liberty for many years the choice and prime young officers of the army—the Rileys, the Kearneys, the Sydney Johnstons—who from time to time were stationed at that post. The wives and daughters of officers went there for shopping purposes. The sons of officers were often sent to Liberty for academic education. The officers of the fort and their wives and daughters were almost as much a part of the social life of the town, as freely united in public amusements, balls, parties and the like, as its inhabitants themselves. From the union of local intellect with the brilliance of the army the society of Liberty became exceptionally charming and elegant.

Into such a society and into the midst of such a people Col. Doniphan went from Lexington in 1833. He was young, ambitious, highly cultured, and his mind expanded with ease to meet the magnitude of each new occasion. The faculty of ready, powerful and tempestuous speech, the flashes of brilliant thought, had come to him. Already the people of the state had recognized in him the orator. The people of Clay County received him with open hearts.

From 1830 to 1860 he continued in the active practice of his profession. His fame was greatest as a criminal lawyer, and during that period there was no criminal cause of magnitude in north west Missouri in which he was not retained for the defence. He never prosecuted. The reputation of a great advocate usually absorbs that of the counsellor. And this was true to a greater degree, perhaps, sixty years ago than now, because then the jury was more often demanded. He was employed to make the threat, the decisive, argument on the side by which he was retained.

No client would think for a moment of excusing him from speaking. He was employed and paid to speak—he must speak. A silent Doniphan in a cause would have meant defeat anticipated. As a natural result of this, the work and labour of the cause, the preparation of the pleadings, the gathering of the testimony, the interrogation of the witnesses, etc., devolved on his associate counsel. Occasionally, in examining witnesses, he would interject some far-reaching question. In the councils of war which precede great trials, his view of the line of defence or attack was always adopted. He saw by a flash of intuition the strong points.

Not one of his oratorical efforts as a criminal or civil lawyer has been preserved. Opinion, therefore, of their power and splendour can only be formed from old tradition. All traditions and opinions concur as to their singular brevity, wonderful compression, vast force and dazzling brilliance. I will merely call attention to two of his orations in criminal defences and give one opinion in each. They are that in defence of Thomas Turnham, indicted in the Clay Circuit Court for the murder of Hayes and tried in November, 1844, which resulted in his conviction of manslaughter in the fourth degree, with a fine of $100; and that of John H. Harper, indicted in the Jackson Circuit Court for the murder of Meredith, and tried in Platte Circuit Court in November, 1847, whither the case had been taken by change of venue. which resulted in Harper's acquittal. There can hardly be a doubt that Turnham's case was one of murder. After great pressure, he was acquitted to bail and his bond fixed at $8,000, an enormous amount in those days. Col. Doniphan was constantly afraid that his client would disappear.

The prisoner's father, the late Maj. Joel Turnham, of Clay County, was a stern, old-fashioned man, "more an antique Roman than a Dane," plainly educated, well advised, however, as to all current events, of strong, penetrating sense, familiar with the great speakers of Missouri and Kentucky, possessed of a will and courage of adamant; but none the less, not at all conscious of the fact that his was the only name in the state which could be found among the paladins of Richard Cœur de Leon when he charged the Paynim hosts on the plains of Palestine. Everything melted away before Col. Doniphan's oratory. At the conclusion of the speech Maj. Turnham was asked what he thought of Doniphan's speech, and his answer was: "Sir, Aleck Doniphan spoke only forty minutes, but he said everything."

The case of Harper more easily admitted of defence. Meredith had—

Loved not wisely, but too well.

Harper believed, whether with or without good reason, that Meredith had invaded the sanctity of his home. Such a circumstance in the hands of a genius like Col. Doniphan's was sufficient to enable him to stir to the uttermost all of the passions and to "call spirits from the vasty deep." The occasion was great. He had returned only a few months before from his wonderful Mexican campaign, and the whole country was full of his glory. Everybody—lawyers and all,—had gathered in Platte City.—where the case was tried,—to hear him, and expectation of his eloquence was on tiptoe. By universal agreement he even surpassed expectation. The late James N. Burnes, of St. Joseph, (then of Weston) heard it, and declared that it determined him to become a lawyer. He, also, declared that he had never heard or read any speech in defence of a criminal which equalled Col. Doniphan's in that case.

Anyone who did not know Col. Doniphan intimately, and who saw him in his prime, or even in his latter years, would have supposed, from the largeness of his frame, the freshness of his complexion, and his erect bearing, that he was a man of vast physical strength and endurance. The exact converse was true. He was physically, one of the most delicate of men and least able to endure exposure or excessive or protracted strain. His whole life was one long struggle against bodily infirmity, and the world knew it not. As a consequence, the prodigious strain on the brain in the delivery of his argument in each of the Turnham and Harper cases, causing excessive cerebral excitement,—a flame of thought, scorching his nervous system,—threw him into a dangerous fever from which he could not be released by the skill of his physicians for several weeks.

The same result occurred in others of his great oratorical efforts. I am perfectly satisfied his consciousness of his physical delicacy acted as a detersive on his ambition and prevented him from seeking those advancements which his friends wished and expected, he fearing that on great and momentous occasions,—occasions demanding extraordinary and prolonged mental effort,—his physical man would yield to the pressure, and he be rendered incapable of meeting expectation.

Before 1836, the lines between whiggery and democracy, or locofocoism, had been clearly drawn. Col. Doniphan came from Kentucky an ardent Whig. He had been politically trained in the school of Harry of the West, of whose vast genius he was, througout life, a most unqualified admirer. Politics in those days had warmth as well as now. Every foot of ground was fought over by the contending parties. In 1836, the Whigs of Clay County demanded that he should become a candidate for the legislature. He acceded to their demand, and was elected. The same facts occurred in 1840, and yet, again, in 1854. In the legislature of 1854, he was the Whig nominee for U. S. senator, and received their unbroken vote.

On December 2 1st, 1837, Col. Doniphan was married to Miss Elizabeh Jane Thornton, of Clay County. It was a perfect union of heart and intellect. She was a highly intellectual, cultivated woman, and her grace of manner and charm in conversation made her the delight of society. Save when public duty or business imperatively demanded it, he and she were constantly united. At home or abroad they were together. They were both insatiable readers, and their evenings in literature will always stir delightful thoughts in the memories of their friends. He knew and loved no place like home, and neither the mystery of lodges nor the joviality of clubs had any power to draw him thence. Heaven withdrew her from him in 1873, but it was decreed that he should remain a pilgrim many years thereafter before he felt the stroke of the invisible spectre—

And sought his love amid the Elysian field.

Of his marriage there were born only two children—both sons. They were youths of rare intellectual promise, and their father might well hope to prolong his life and fame in those of his children. One of them died from accidental poison, at Liberty in 1853, and the other beneath the angry waves of a West Virginia brook in 1858. From blows so severe as these, it can be well understood why the life of Col. Doniphan, during more than thirty years before its close, was void of ambition.

Of the Mormon war in 1838, I will simply state that Col. Doniphan was present, in command of a brigade of state militia, at the surrender of Joe Smith, the so-called prophet, at Far West in Caldwell county, and afterward defended him in the criminal proceedings which were instituted against him and other Mormons.

In 1846 the war with Mexico began. In May of that year, Governor Edwards requested Col. Doniphan to assist him in raising troops, in the western counties of the state, for the volunteer service. He acceded to the request. The enthusiasm of the people was extremely high, and, in a week or so, the eight companies of men had volunteered, which, upon organisation at Fort Leavenworth, formed the famous 1st Regiment of Missouri Mounted Volunteers. The counties which furnished those companies were Jackson, Lafayette, Clay, Saline, Franklin, Cole, Howard and Callaway. Col. Doniphan volunteered as a private in the company from Clay. The desire to volunteer was so great among the counties that each of the companies was much overfull.

That from Clay numbered 118 men, rank and file. The subject of this sketch was elected colonel of the regiment almost by acclamation. There never was in the service of the United States a regiment of finer material. It was composed of individuals from the best families in the state, and they were young men in the prime of life, equal, physically and mentally, to every duty of the soldier. They were, mainly, the sons of pioneers of Missouri, and had the courage and manliness, and possessed the endurance and virtues of their fathers. This regiment formed a portion of the column known as the Army of the West, commanded by that chivalric soldier. Gen. Stephen W . Kearney. All of the troops of the column rendezvoused at Fort Leavenworth. The volunteers having undergone a few weeks of drilling, the Army of the West commenced its march to Santa Fe on June 26th, 1846.

It would be impossible to express in words the feelings, apprehensions and hopes of the people and of those volunteers when Gen. Kearney's army moved to the conquest of northern Mexico. The knowledge of the American people then of Mexico was very limited. The people of Missouri knew more than any others, for their traders, at least, during over twenty years previously, had laboriously tracked and retracked the dangerous trail from Independence to Santa Fe, and thence to Chihuahua. The geographies of that dayt—old Olney and Mitchell—showed little beyond outlines delineating Mexico and the countries west of Missouri. They indicated, however, very clearly, the Great American Desert, extending and wide between Missouri and Mexico. The regions between our state and Mexico were Indian country and dangerous, and those beyond were Indian and Mexican, and still more dangerous. Our volunteers must have felt that every mile of their march would reveal surprises and wonders. And we may liken their expectation of encountering the marvellous to that of Sir Francis Drake, when, three hundred years ago, he weighed his anchors at Portsmouth and turned the prow of his ship towards the South Sea.

On August 18, 1846, Gen. Kearney's army entered Santa Fe without firing a gun. In November, 1846, Col. Doniphan, with his regiment, was ordered into the country of the Navajo Indians, on the western slope of the Rocky Mountains, to overawe or chastise them. He completed this movement with great celerity. His soldiers toiled through snows three feet deep on the crests and eastern slope of the mountains. Having accomplished the object of the exp)edition, concluding a satisfactory treay with the Indians, he returned to the Rio del Norte, and, on the banks of that stream, collected and refreshed his men, preparatory to effecting what was then intended to be a junction with Gen. Wool. He was there reinforced by two batteries of light artillery. In December, 1846, he turned the faces of his little column to the south, and put it in motion towards Chihuahua. In quick succession followed his brilliant and decisive victories at Bracito and Sacramento, the capture of Chihuahua, the plunge of his little army into the unknown country between Chihuahua and Saltillo, and its emergence in triumph at the latter city.

After his arrival at Saltillo, inasmuch as the period of enlistment of his men would soon expire, his regiment was ordered home. Its march, therefore, was continued to Matamoras, where it took shipping to New Orleans. The men of the regiment, having been discharged at New Orleans, arrived at home about July 1st. 1847. The march of this regiment from Fort Leavenworth to Santa Fe, Chihuahua, Saltillo and Matamoras—a distance of nearly 3,600 miles—is called Doniphan's Expedition.

On his return from Mexico he at once resumed the practice of his profession.

In 1854 a fact occurred which fully illustrates the belief of the people of Clay County—a belief which extended all over the state—in his universal ability and fitness for any station, high or low. On February 24th, 1853, the act was passed by our legislature which provided for the organisation, support and government of the public schools, and which thereafter set apart twenty-five *per cent.* annually, of the state revenue for their support. In November, 1853, it became necessary for the County Court of Clay County to appoint a "commissioner of common schools" for the county. By a singular unanimity and without thought of anyone else, the people of the county asked Col. Doniphan to accept the position, and petitioned the County Court to appoint him.

He accepted the appointment, saying he ought to do so because the people of the county had done everything they could for him. He retained the position near a year, and gave, by his energy and encouragement, an impetus to the public school system in the county which was never checked. During his incumbency, and through his inspiration, a teacher's institute was organised and held in the county, which was the first one ever held in Missouri.

In January, 1861, he was appointed a member of the peace conference, which assembled at Washington with a view to prevention of civil war. During his absence in attendance on that body, he was elected a member of the state convention called by the legislature, January 21st, 1861. In the convention he maintained the position of a conservative union man, and did not permit himself to lose sight either of the supremacy of the constitution or the reserved rights of the states. In 1863,—during; the heat of the civil war,—he removed from Liberty to St. Louis. Family reasons compelling, in 1868, he removed from St. Louis to Richmond, Missouri, and resided at the latter place until his death.

The oratory of Col. Doniphan at the bar constitutes only a part of the basis of his fame as an orator. From his immigration to Missouri until the close of 1860, in every canvass he responded to the wishes of the political party to which he was attached, and on the hustings in various parts of our state, he advocated and defended his party's principles in addresses of surpassing logic and flaming eloquence. Enormous crowds met him wherever he spoke, and the people would never weary of listening to his accents. Ami this was not all. His addresses on various public occasions, educational, social and patriotic, from his arrival in our state until 1872, were numerous. And yet of all his magnificent orations, so far as I know, but two remain complete, and they were delivered on occasions social or festive. In so far as the records of time—the gravings of history and legislative proceedings extend, his name is secure. But what of the power and magnificence of his oratory? It rests only in tradition.

It must always be a matter of regret that not in equal degree are the efforts of genius transmitted to after times. The mighty historians and poets are secure in their immortality. Homer, Virgil, Milton, Thucydides, Tacitus, Gibbon, will always be read. The great Greek historian, in sixty pages of moderate size, sketched the Athenian expedition against Syracuse, the embarkation, the passage of the sea, the debarkation, the beleaguering of the city, the assault, the repulse, the retreat, the overthrow and capture, with an amazing clearness and power which have made his place in the temple of fame as stable as the world itself.

The sculptor, secure in his marble, may reasonably hope that the visions of loveliness or majesty, born of his brain. may transmit his name some thousands of years. Even the painter is assured that the divine conceptions which he has limned may be admired and judged by the eye—and his name repeated—for a few centuries after he has passed away. It is said—

The actor, only, shrinks from Time's award.

After the revolutions of eighteen centuries, we know the name of
Roscius, and but little more.

The grace of action—the adapted mien,
Faithful as nature lo the varied scene:
The expressive glance—whose subtle comment draws
Entranced attention and a mute applause:
Gesture that marks with force and feeling fraught,
A sense in silence and a will in thought.
Harmonious speech whose pure and liquid tone
Gives verse a music, scarce confessed its own,—

How can these be conveyed to the mind of another by the force;
of words? In so far as action is concerned, what is true of the actor
is equally true of the orator. Who would attempt to paint Alexander
W. Doniphan in the torrent of his eloquence on some momentous
occasion? Who would attempt to convey an idea, by language, of his
grand person, towering above all the people—his eyes burning; with
tenfold the lustre of diamonds—the sweep of his arm when raised
to enforce some splendid conception—his pure and flute-like voice,
thrilling every bosom like electricity—his rapid, explanatory sketch
of preliminary matters, each word a picture to the life—his conclu-
sions, remorseless as death—his flaming excursions into every realm
of fancy—his wit, his humour, his pathos, his passionate energy of
utterance? All this must forever remain unknown, save only to those
who were so fortunate as to have heard his oratory when he was in
his prime.

In the absence of mental efforts preserved—which can be studied
and meditated—in order to a proper measurement of the intellect of
Alexander W. Doniphan, and a due appreciation of his genius, someone is needed who was familiar with him in his prime, that is to say
from 1835 to 1855, and who was himself of mature mind during that
period. I heard none of his great efforts in criminal causes. I heard
a few of them in civil cases. My opinion of his intellect and genius
is formed from a copious and sure tradition, a few of his political
and public efforts, worthy, in my judgement, of the reputation of the
greatest of American orators, the expressions of men of high intellects
themselves, and familiar and intimate observation of the action of his
mind since my earliest recollection.

Great men only appear after long intervals. Eight centuries prior to the Saviour of men, the mightiest poet of the antique world sang the tale of Troy; more than seven centuries elapsed before the Mantuan bard sang of Æneas; and sixteen centuries must then roll away ere time was prepared for the birth of Shakespeare. Three hundred years intervened between the great Macedonian conqueror and imperial Caesar; and eighteen hundred between Caesar and Napoleon. Between Thucydides and Tacitus are near five hundred, and between Tacitus and Gibbon, near seventeen hundred years. From Demosthenes to Cicero were three hundred years, and from Cicero to the majestic line of Chatham. Sheridan, Burke, Fox, Clay, Webster, Calhoun and Doniphan were eighteen hundred years.

The genius of Col. Doniphan can only be estimated, in all its height, depth, breadth and splendour, by one who had known him in his prime, and under all circumstances and conditions. He must have known him in the field of Sacramento, when, six hundred miles in the enemy's country, he led his little army of Missourians to the assault of works manned by four times their number; when, in the defence of some prisoner, charged with the greatest offense known to the law, in order to succeed, he called into action all of his intellectual powers, and thundered and lightened in addressing the jury; when, before a great audience of his fellow-citizens, assembled to hear him on some momentous occasion, he brought into play the whole range of his stores of thought, sentiment, eloquence and wit, transported his auditors from grave to gay, from tears to mirth, with a certain divine ease and rapidity, and moulded their opinions and hearts to his will with a thoroughness only possible to the greatest orator; and when, the cares of the forum and politics laid aside, at his own or a friend's fireside, or. beneath the spreading branches of some monarch of the forest, he relaxed his gigantic intellect to the needs and uses of social converse. and charmed all listeners with a flow of wisdom, humour, anecdote— strong, yet airy and graceful—so rich, so varied, so flashing, that it would have made the literary fortune of a dozen writers.

It is and has been the clear opinion of all who have known him well, that, in all the qualities of the loftiest intellect,—breadth of vision. foresight which could farthest in advance discern matters that would come to pass, intuitive perception, rapidity of determination, sharp analysis, precision of judgment, corroding logic, subtlety of thought, richness and variety of fancy, aptness of illustration, powerful and unfailing memory, compression of words, ease in mental action, and intense, nervervous, crystalline and electrical language,—indeed in all the elements of genius,—he has never had a superior in America.

This opinion I will accentuate by that of a man well able to judge and whose opportunities to form a safe judgement, were better than those of any man. living or dead,—I mean the late Gen. David R. Atchison. Gen. Atchison was a man of education, of .strong, judicial intellect, trained thought, had been senator from our state from 1843 to 1855, and his observation of and experience among men had been of the largest. A few years prior to his and Col. Doniphan's death, he said to me: "I was familiar with the city of Washington in my early manhood. I knew all the great men of our country in the earlier days—Clay, Webster, Calhoun, John Quincy Adams, Clayton, Crittenden and others. I have presided in the United States Senate when Clay Webster and Calhoun sat before me. I knew Aleck Doniphan familiarly, intimately, since 1830, and I tell you, sir, when he was in his prime, I heard him climb higher than any of them."

But higher than Col. Doniphan's gifts of mind were those of his heart—his marvellous humanity.

A Roman said—

Vietrix causa Diis plaenit. sed vieta Catoni.

The Gods loved the victors, but Cato the vanquished. The nobility of this sentiment is the more to be admired because of the rarity of expressions of sympathy by victors for the vanquished in the classic world. He knew that Roman conquest meant the march of the legions to the devoted country—the overthrow and slaughter of opposing armies—the siege and sack of cities—the desecration of temples—the capture of spoils of silver and gold and men—captives following at the chariot wheels of the triumphant general—the sale of men and women into slavery—the *prætor* and tax-gatherer, following the sword—the exactions and extortions—and his great, compassionate heart overflowed with pity for the enslaved, the feeble, and unhappy.

Like Cato, Col. Doniphan had this wonderful compassion for the weak, defenceless and miserable only that it was broadened and made; more tender, gracious and personal by Christian culture. To compassion, he united, in the highest degree, courtesy and modesty and, therefore, he was accessible to all alike the rich, the poor, the high, the low, the statesman and the peasant. No one who knew him will fail to remember with what charm he drew all to him, nor how a child, a humble slave, a modest woman, a poor labourer in the field or shop, could address him with as much ease and as free from embarrassment as the proudest potentate in the land. There was no oppression in his presence. The great man was forgotten in the genial friend and faithful counsellor.

In the varied circumstances of his life, Col. Doniphan exerted a very great influence. In parliamentary bodies, he did this mainly through social impress and personal contact. He was wonderfully fascinating in conversation, and his society was sought with the greatest eagerness wherever he went. The people all over Missouri thronged around him when he was among them, and, it seemed, they never could sufficiently drink in his utterances.

Perhaps there never was a more delightful or instructive and amusing conversationalist. His faculties of generalisation, perception and analysis were very remarkable. His temperament was poetic, even romantic, but guarded by fine taste and the most delicate sense of the ludicrous. Indeed, his mind was so well organised, so nicely balanced, its machinery so happily fitted, its stores of information so well digested and so completely incorporated into his every-day thought, that its riches, without effort, apparently, flowed or flashed forth on all occasions, and placed all it touched in a flood of light.

His personal appearance was truly imposing and magnificent. His was of the grandest type of manly beauty. A stranger would not have failed to instantly note his presence in any assemblage. In height, he was six feet and four inches. His frame was proportioned to his height, and was full without the appearance of obesity. His face approached the Grecian ideal very closely the essential variance being in the nose, which was aquiline without severity. His forehead was high, full and square; his eyes of the brightest hazel; and his lips symmetrical and smiling. When young, his complexion was extremely fair and delicate, and his hair sandy.

At the peace conference in 1861, when introduced to Mr. Lincoln, the latter said to him: "And this is the Col. Doniphan who made the wild march against the Comanches and Mexicans. You are the only man I ever met who. in appearance, came up to my previous expectation."

Col. Doniphan died at Richmond. Missouri, August 8th. 1887, and was buried at Liberty Missouri, with his wife and sons.

He united with the Christian Church in 1859, and died in its faith.

NOTE

Henry Tillery was, also, a private in Company C (see preface), but in setting up the names of Company C, his was accidentally overlooked.

www.ingramcontent.com/pod-product-compliance
Lightning Source LLC
Chambersburg PA
CBHW032017090426
42741CB00006B/626